slide:ology

**THE ART AND SCIENCE
OF CREATING GREAT
PRESENTATIONS**

Praise for slide:ology

"Now that Nancy has published this book, what's your excuse for your long, boring, and useless presentations?"

Guy Kawasaki
Co-founder of Alltop, author of *The Art of the Start*

"This is a breathtaking book! Nancy has written a long-overdue scholar's guide to the art and science of presentation. If you're serious about this craft, it's hard to imagine doing your best work without studying this book first. Study it, memorize it, share it."

Seth Godin
Author, *Really Bad PowerPoint*

"The most successful TED speakers spread brilliant ideas following the timeless principles in this invaluable book. It's a safe bet we'll be sending this book to all future presenters just as soon as they confirm!"

Tom Rielly
TED Conferences

"I've been begging Nancy for years to put her 20 years of wisdom and experience into print form, and she has delivered beyond all expectations with *slide:ology*. Any presenter will savor this encyclopedia of slide design, filled with page after page of theory, principles, anecdotes, examples and real-world case studies. You'll keep it by your laptop for years as a reference. There's no excuse to use the same old boring bullet points—it's time to start unlocking the power of your own visual stories!"

Cliff Atkinson
Author, *Beyond Bullet Points*

"At last, someone has assembled a much-needed successor to the Tufte trilogy!"

Raymond Nasr
Former Director of Communications, Google

"This is a book for absorbing, as you would good wine or great jazz. It will go down smoothly and transform you into a better presenter. I look forward to a global elevation of presentation quality, the source of which we'll trace right back here."

Ric Bretschneider
Senior Program Manager, Microsoft Office PowerPoint

"If you are ever presenting in a business setting, you MUST have Nancy's book, *slide:ology*. It's more than slides and design—it's about communication and inspiration. And this book will help anyone—beginner or top professional—get to the top of their game. Simply and creatively."

Bert Decker
CEO, Decker Communications, Inc.

"Nancy Duarte gets it. She understands that designing slides for presentations is about providing support for the presenter rather than creating pretty pictures. The exigencies of business all too often push designers to produce slides into the dreaded Presentation-as-Document Syndrome, a hybrid that serves neither purpose; neither fish nor fowl. Nancy has always resisted that push by maintaining the proper role of graphics for her clients; now she has eloquently translated her concepts for her readers. From her opening sentence positioning presentations as the foundation of communication in business, she provides the solid building blocks for effective graphic design."

Jerry Weissman
Author, *The Power Presenter*

"Duarte's simple, unique design approach helps create stories that are memorable."

Robert Haskitt
Director of Marketing, Microsoft Advertising

"*slide:ology* is a beautifully-designed, practical guide to creating visually effective presentations. While referencing the work that has gone on before, Nancy brings a fresh perspective to this inaugural effort. Previous authors have focused on developing great presentations through planning, organization, writing, and speaking skills, but none has focused on the effective use of visuals in presentations. She provides a good balance between theory and application in a book filled with visual examples."

Tom Crawford
CEO, VizThink

slide:ology

**THE ART AND SCIENCE
OF CREATING GREAT
PRESENTATIONS**

NANCY DUARTE

Beijing • Cambridge • Farnham • Köln • Sebastopol • Taipei • Tokyo

slide:ology

The Art and Science of Creating Great Presentations
by Nancy Duarte

Published by O'Reilly Media, Inc. 1005 Gravenstein Highway North,
Sebastopol CA 95472

O'Reilly books may be purchased for educational, business, or sales promotional use. Online editions are also available for most titles *(safari.oreilly.com)*. For more information, contact our corporate/institutional sales department: (800) 998-9938 or *corporate@oreilly.com*.

Executive Editor: Steve Weiss
Managing Editor: Dennis Fitzgerald
Editor: Judy Walthers von Alten
Cover Design: Diandra Macias
Art Director: Diandra Macias
Designer: Michaela Kastlova
Proofreader: Nancy Bell
Indexer: Ted Laux

All images copyright by the author or have been licensed by the author unless otherwise noted.

Print History: First Edition, September 2008

This book uses RepKover™, a durable and flexible lay-flat binding.

ISBN-13: 978-0-596-52234-6
[F]

To my clients, my employees, my family, and my Creator. What a fun ride it's been!

Acknowledgments

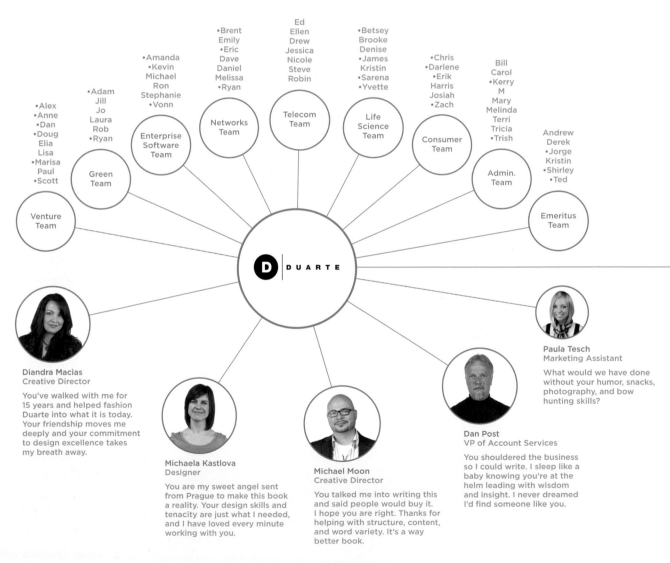

•Alex
•Anne
•Dan
•Doug
Elia
Lisa
•Marisa
Paul
•Scott

Venture Team

•Adam
Jill
Jo
Laura
Rob
•Ryan

Green Team

•Amanda
•Kevin
Michael
Ron
Stephanie
•Vonn

Enterprise Software Team

•Brent
Emily
•Eric
Dave
Daniel
Melissa
•Ryan

Networks Team

Ed
Ellen
Drew
Jessica
Nicole
Steve
Robin

Telecom Team

•Betsey
Brooke
Denise
•James
Kristin
•Sarena
•Yvette

Life Science Team

•Chris
•Darlene
•Erik
Harris
Josiah
•Zach

Consumer Team

Bill
Carol
•Kerry
M
Mary
Melinda
Terri
Tricia
•Trish

Admin. Team

Andrew
Derek
•Jorge
Kristin
•Shirley
•Ted

Emeritus Team

D DUARTE

Diandra Macias
Creative Director

You've walked with me for 15 years and helped fashion Duarte into what it is today. Your friendship moves me deeply and your commitment to design excellence takes my breath away.

Michaela Kastlova
Designer

You are my sweet angel sent from Prague to make this book a reality. Your design skills and tenacity are just what I needed, and I have loved every minute working with you.

Michael Moon
Creative Director

You talked me into writing this and said people would buy it. I hope you are right. Thanks for helping with structure, content, and word variety. It's a way better book.

Dan Post
VP of Account Services

You shouldered the business so I could write. I sleep like a baby knowing you're at the helm leading with wisdom and insight. I never dreamed I'd find someone like you.

Paula Tesch
Marketing Assistant

What would we have done without your humor, snacks, photography, and bow hunting skills?

• *Contributed significantly to book.*

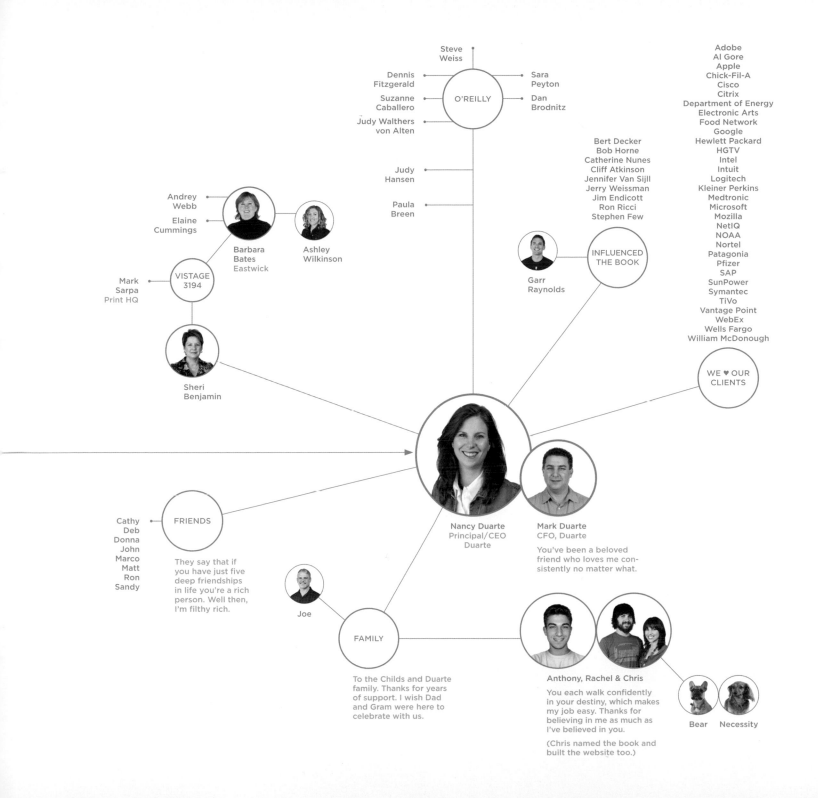

Steve
Weiss

Dennis
Fitzgerald

Suzanne
Caballero

Judy Walthers
von Alten

O'REILLY

Sara
Peyton

Dan
Brodnitz

Adobe
Al Gore
Apple
Chick-Fil-A
Cisco
Citrix
Department of Energy
Electronic Arts
Food Network
Google
Hewlett Packard
HGTV
Intel
Intuit
Logitech
Kleiner Perkins
Medtronic
Microsoft
Mozilla
NetIQ
NOAA
Nortel
Patagonia
Pfizer
SAP
SunPower
Symantec
TiVo
Vantage Point
WebEx
Wells Fargo
William McDonough

Judy
Hansen

Paula
Breen

Bert Decker
Bob Horne
Catherine Nunes
Cliff Atkinson
Jennifer Van Sijll
Jerry Weissman
Jim Endicott
Ron Ricci
Stephen Few

Andrey
Webb

Elaine
Cummings

Barbara
Bates
Eastwick

Ashley
Wilkinson

INFLUENCED
THE BOOK

Garr
Raynolds

Mark
Sarpa
Print HQ

VISTAGE
3194

WE ♥ OUR
CLIENTS

Sheri
Benjamin

Nancy Duarte
Principal/CEO
Duarte

Mark Duarte
CFO, Duarte

You've been a beloved
friend who loves me con-
sistently no matter what.

Cathy
Deb
Donna
John
Marco
Matt
Ron
Sandy

FRIENDS

They say that if
you have just five
deep friendships
in life you're a rich
person. Well then,
I'm filthy rich.

Joe

FAMILY

To the Childs and Duarte
family. Thanks for years
of support. I wish Dad
and Gram were here to
celebrate with us.

Anthony, Rachel & Chris

You each walk confidently
in your destiny, which makes
my job easy. Thanks for
believing in me as much as
I've believed in you.

(Chris named the book and
built the website too.)

Bear   Necessity

Contents

Foreword

In 1987 my wife, Nancy, was pleading with me to send out my resume and get a "real" job. She wasn't too convinced that my business idea of creating graphics on my brand new MacPlus 512k personal computer would ever take off. But much to our surprise it did. Up to this point business presentations were delivered in 35mm format and created by specialized professional designers. Presentation software was developed intentionally to cut the designer out of the process so presentations could be created by anyone with a computer. Including us.

The software was indeed a great invention. But eliminating design from the mix was a mistake. Like Thoreau said, "We've become the tool of our tools."

My daughter Rachel created the story to the right to help articulate in pictures what the problem is with presentations today. This fabulous story breaks down into dry bullet points that risk losing the listener in the woods, just like Red Riding Hood. Somehow the ability to tell a good story is lost when presentation software is added into the mix.

The tool isn't going away and the corporate stories that need telling today are some of the most innovative and inspiring in history. Yet these stories get buried in a presentation framework that challenges patience instead of stimulating creativity.

For this cause, Nancy has put her heart and soul for over two years into writing this book. It's been pasted up around the house, and pored over when "on vacation." I often woke up in the middle of the night with her side of the bed empty, able to hear the faint clicking of her keyboard while she hammered out just one more idea for the book.

From the earliest draft I saw, I thought, "this book is brilliant." It will change you as a presenter if you take to heart the principles contained within. *slide:ology* is destined to become the desk reference for building effective presentations and is a must read for all who present.

I'm immensely proud of what Nancy has accomplished. She has taken her expertise and many years of experience working with some of the best brands and thought leaders in the world, and compiled it as a masterly work of art and science.

Get ready to be inspired!

Mark Duarte
Founder/ CFO, Duarte

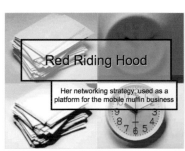

Brief History of Visual Aids

15000
BCE

3000
BCE

500
BCE

950
CE

1350
CE

1845
CE

Cave Paintings

The 2,000 images found in the caves at Lascaux, France narrate stories through character, sequence, and motion. The oldest evidence the world has of visual storytelling, the paintings demonstrate early reliance on using images to convey meaning.

Egyptian Murals

Large, pictographic murals communicate complex ideas to crowds of thousands. Hieroglyphic symbols—functioning as both representative images and phonetic components—augment larger images to blend visual and verbal communication.

Public Speaking

The Greeks pioneer the study and practice of oratory and logography. Centuries later, Ars Oratoria (the art of public speaking) is a mark of professional competence in Rome, especially among politicians and lawyers.

Stained Glass Windows

Before the printing press, the Roman Catholic Church conveyed stories of saints and biblical characters to a mostly illiterate public through the colorful medium of stained glass. The messages stick.

Bar Graphs

Bishop Nicole Oresme creates a "Proto-Bar Graph" for plotting variables in a coordinate system. Thankfully, he lacks distracting, modern textures.

Comic Strips

Swiss artist Rudolphe Töpffer develops the forerunner to today's modern comic strips: he tells complete stories using frames that contain both images and text.

When you think of presentations, your immediate thoughts probably travel only as far back as 1987—the beginning of the PowerPoint era. If you broaden your perspective, you might recall an age of 35mm slides and flip charts—the latter half of the last century. And though the means and methods have changed over time, the messages by and large have not: you recount stories, present new information, strive to change others' minds. The world is wired for visual as well as verbal communication. Don't believe it? Consider this timeline:

1945 CE

Overhead Projector

Police begin using overhead projectors for their identification work, quickly followed by the military, educators, and businesses.

1950 CE

35mm Slide Presentations

The 35mm slide projector enables professionals to communicate ideas sequentially to larger audiences. The pioneering 35mm slide firm Genagraphics charges from $300 to $1500 per proprietary slide.

1987 CE

PowerPoint

The click heard 'round the world: PowerPoint 1.0 debuts for the Macintosh. Suddenly everyone can design slides. Little consideration is given to whether or not this is a good idea.

1992 CE

Pervasive PC

PCs sit on every desktop in the workplace and high-stakes business communications evolve from printed documents to digital presentations. The 35mm slide companies go extinct almost overnight.

2003 CE

Cognitive Style of PowerPoint

Edward Tufte authors "The Cognitive Style of PowerPoint." In it, he suggests that PowerPoint impaired the quality of the engineers' investigative analysis on the Columbia Space Shuttle when it was gravely impacted by debris.

2007 CE

An Inconvenient Truth

Al Gore raises environmental consciousness, wins an Academy Award, and receives the Nobel Peace Prize for telling a compelling story about climate change with little more than a slide show.

Nearly all men can stand adversity, but if you want to test a man's character, give him power. ^Point

Abraham Lincoln

Introduction

Presentations have become the de facto business communication tool. Companies are started, products are launched, climate systems are saved—possibly based on the quality of presentations. Likewise, ideas, endeavors, and even careers can be cut short due to ineffective communication. Out of the millions of presentations delivered each day, only a small percentage are delivered well—and as a society, we've come to expect it.

We groan when we have to attend a meeting with the slide deck as the star.

Whether you're a CEO, senior manager, or educator, you create presentations that have incredibly high stakes. Stock value, sales revenue, career promotions, and behavior changes are all influenced by presentations every day. But our lack of training in visual communication has enabled presentations to be blamed for shuttle disasters, low test scores, and SEC scandals. The two guys who invented the software were even quoted in the *Wall Street Journal* as saying, "the best way to paralyze an opposition army is to ship it PowerPoint."

Presentation software is the first application broadly adopted by professionals that requires people to think visually.

Unfortunately, most people never make the jump from verbal expression—which is what we were all taught in school—to effective visual expression, which is neither easy nor natural. Slides are thus stranded in a no man's land where the general population doesn't know how to effectively produce or deliver them. Yet when a presentation is developed and delivered well, it is one of our most powerful communication tools in the world. Just look at the tipping point Al Gore created for climate change because of his slide show, or the frenzied anticipation when Steve Jobs unveils new products.

We can keep blaming the software for the putrid output, but in reality we need to take responsibility. As communicators, learning to create visual stories that connect with our audience is becoming imperative—especially in light of global competitive pressure.

This book covers how to create ideas, translate them into pictures, display them well, and then deliver them in your own natural way. It is NOT a PowerPoint manual. You'll find no pull-down menus or application shortcuts, instead there are timeless principles to ingest and apply. It's a reference book that you'll want to open often. This book will teach you "why".

The pages are structured with one thought per spread, and the flow of the book follows the stages of presentation development from idea generation through delivery. When you see the www symbol on a page, that means that there is additional supporting content for that page on the book's website, www.slideology.com.

I've had the privilege of working with the greatest brands in the world and have pulled years of best practices into this book. Some people think I'm crazy to give away 20 years of expertise. So why would I do this? I'm hoping it will spark change. Historically, change occurs when a new ideology catches fire and permeates a culture, and then the people take action. Look closely and you'll see that the word ideology is embedded in the book name. My hope is that you will change your approach, stance, and ideologies about the power a great slide has to facilitate epiphanies.

slide:ology will revolutionize presentation communications. It can change how you plan, ideate, create, and deliver a presentation. Once you harness the concepts around visual storytelling, mediocre slides will not be good enough any more. You'll have the resolve to challenge the status quo and set a higher communication benchmark for yourself and your organization.

Every presenter has the potential to be great; every presentation is high stakes; and every audience deserves the absolute best.

And maybe, just maybe, creating great slides will help you be more confident, cause audiences to sit up and take notice, and ultimately silence the critics of what I think is the most powerful communication medium on Earth.

Warning: This book is not for you if you want to remain a marginal corporate citizen.

all for the cause!

All work examples in this book were created by Duarte except for a few examples in the last chapter from Andy Proehl, Garr Reynolds, Scott Harrison, John Ortberg, Jill Bolte-Taylor, and Sky McCloud.

CHAPTER 1

Creating a New Slide Ideology

Don't Commit Career Suislide

We are all inherently visual communicators. Consider kindergarten: crayons, finger paints, and clay propelled our expression, not word processors or spreadsheets.

Yet, the stories you told with these limited means were at least as good—perhaps better—than what you can accomplish with today's technology. For instance, the following image was painted by Lucas, the son of a friend of mine. On first glance it looks like meaningless globs of paint. But Lucas' story is about a penguin party, and in that context, the images make brilliant sense. The greater message here is that stories are how people understand and relate to the world, and they naturally associate those stories with appropriate imagery.

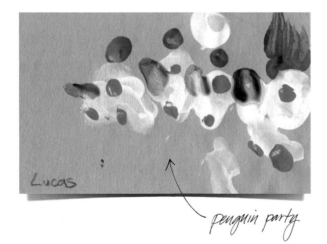

penguin party

Unfortunately, somewhere, at some time, someone probably told you that you weren't very good at drawing. And, after looking around and comparing yourself to other kids in the classroom, you probably consented, threw in the towel, and decided that piano lessons or football might prove a better bet for primary education glory.

Now, as an adult, you may not try anymore—at least in the visual realm. This is ironic considering that your employers and colleagues assess you by how well you communicate—a skill that is reflected in annual reviews, pay increases, promotions, and even your popularity. Effective communication is a job requirement now, whether you're trying to beat competitors, communicate vision, demonstrate thought leadership, raise capital, or otherwise change the world. And like it or not, your profession likely requires you to communicate using a visual tool, regardless of your proficiency or training in this medium. Business schools in particular drill their students in management, accounting, and technology, but few offer anything approaching Design 101—the one thing that combines creative thinking, analytics, data assimilation, and the inherent ability to express oneself visually.

Others have noted the Catch-22 pressure of being able to communicate well visually without the proper training. Marcus Buckingham, on a conference call about his book *Go Put Your Strengths to Work,* recounted his own experience this way:

"I figured out pretty quickly that most of the sales people I was working with weren't very good at putting together PowerPoint presentations. I took it upon myself to become as expert as I could. Not that I'm some genius now, but I can put together a great presentation really quickly and effectively. And it made me a more valuable asset."

Marcus Buckingham
Author, *Go Put Your Strengths to Work*

Closer to home, my brother-in-law, a retired lieutenant commander in the U.S. Navy, recalled that presenting less than optimum slides made promotion difficult. Twenty years ago, no one would have guessed that knowledge of this visual medium would be so pervasive or so important. Indeed, International Communications Industries Association concluded from a recent study that very few presentation professionals themselves have had any graphic design training. And these are the people who work at large companies and build slides full time!

Making bad slides is easy, and it will negatively impact your career. Invest in your slides, but invest in your own visual skills as well. The alternative is to inadvertently commit career suislide.

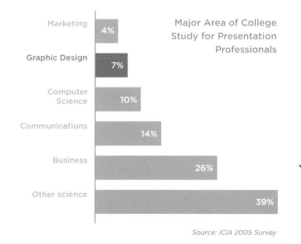

Major Area of College Study for Presentation Professionals

Marketing 4%
Graphic Design 7%
Computer Science 10%
Communications 14%
Business 26%
Other science 39%

Source: ICIA 2005 Survey

A Case for Presentations

Corporations spend hundreds of millions of dollars on advertising, marketing, and PR to attract and retain consumers. They run TV ads, place banner ads, erect billboards, write articles, and dispatch massive amounts of annoying junk mail, all to persuade customers of the superiority of their products and services. Sometimes this is enough; consumers are convinced and accounts are won. But other times, these expensive means are merely a prelude to a personal engagement—one that will depend on the effectiveness of a presentation to seal the deal.

Now, consider the disparity between the content, design, and production values of that $100 million campaign, and the slide show residing on your laptop. Consider also that this slide show may be the last engagement you have with your customers before they make a purchase decision. From an experiential standpoint, few things could be more anticlimactic than a massive campaign followed by an unorganized, unmoving presentation that might not be relevant to what the audience needs from you or the company.

How is it that companies became so focused on a grandiose approach to marketing yet so reluctant to spend even a fraction of the time needed to create a great presentation?

Truth be told, the reason many organizations relegate slides to the bottom of the marketing food chain has to do with how they approach brand.

Many companies have forgotten—or simply never realized—what branding is. Rather than a name or logo or tagline that reflects what a company thinks of itself, brand is what a company stands for in the hearts and minds of its customers; to be successful, the company must have an emotional connection with the consumer.

Similarly, presentations all too often reflect the agenda of the presenter rather than build a connection with the audience. This is unfortunate because presentations could be considered the last branding frontier, in terms of both the attention paid to them and where they fit in the sales cycle.

In many instances, presentations are the last impression a customer has of a company before closing a business deal.

Indeed, it wouldn't take much for any company to stand out from its competitors if it paid some respect to its brand—and its audience—through its presentations.

The collective (mis)use of this presentation medium has informed everyone's opinion of it. Some people simply don't understand how powerful and moving a presentation can be.

Let's go fix that.

Presentations are a tool for high-stakes internal and external communications. This medium will influence many of your important constituents and the impression they develop of you and your company.

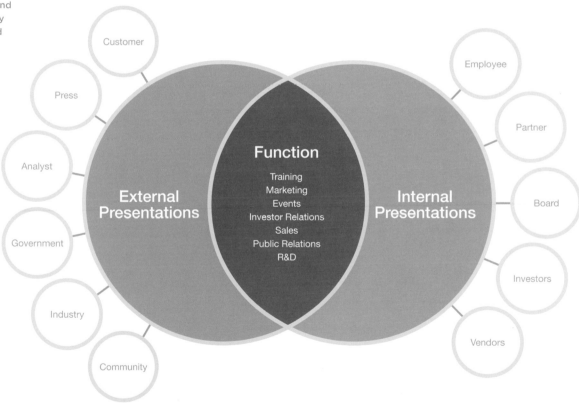

So Where Do You Begin?

Use the right tool the right way.

At a certain point, the number of words on a slide prevents it from being a visual aid. You've been there. The audience is reading the slides instead of paying attention to the presenter, the presenter is reading the slides instead of connecting with the audience, and the whole endeavor would have been better served through a well-composed document or even an email.

Unfortunately, the negative habits that lead to this kind of presentation style are deeply rooted and difficult to change. But consider this: audiences will either listen to what a presenter is saying or read the slides themselves. They won't do both. Why? People tend to focus on one stream of verbal communication at a time—listening and reading are conflicting activities.

On the other hand, it's natural for people to simultaneously pay attention to both verbal and visual communication. That's why great slides serve as a visual aid that reinforces the speaker's message.

However, the heavy use of text occasionally might be appropriate, but in such a case, you should be careful what medium you use. Too often, presentation software is used to create documents. Garr Reynolds, author of *Presentation Zen,* calls these slideuments. So before your next presentation, assess how you've used the application. Did you create a document or a presentation? Either adjust your documents into slides or trust that your audience is smart enough to read and circulate your slides as a document.

"Communication is about getting others to adopt your point of view, to help them understand why you're excited (or sad, or optimistic, or whatever else you are). If all you want to do is create a file of facts and figures, then cancel the meeting and send in a report."

Seth Godin,
Author, *Really Bad PowerPoint*

People will love you for respecting their time enough to use the media appropriately.

This book primarily focuses on presentations that are on the far right of this spectrum.

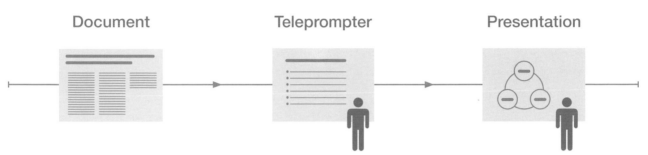

Document

Dense content in a presentation intended as a discussion document or whitepaper; a slideument.

If a slide contains more than 75 words, it has become a document. You can either reduce the amount of content on the slide and put it in the notes, or admit that this is a document and not a presentation. If it is the latter, host a meeting instead of a presentation, and circulate the slideument ahead of time or allow the audience to read it at the start. Then you can use the remainder of the meeting to discuss the content and build action plans.

Teleprompter

Text on the slide functions as a crutch for the presenter. The audience either reads the slides or listens to the presenter.

Presentations with 50 or so words per slide serve as a teleprompter. This less-than-engaging approach often results from a lack of time spent rehearsing the content, and is the default style of many professionals. Unfortunately, presenters who rely on the teleprompter approach also usually turn their backs to the audience. The audience may even perceive such presenters as slow, as the audience reads ahead and has to wait for the presenter to catch up.

Presentation

Slides are effectively used as a visual aid to reinforce the presenter's message.

True presentations focus on the presenter and the visionary ideas and concepts they want to communicate. The slides reinforce the content visually rather than create distraction, allowing the audience to comfortably focus on both. It takes an investment of time on the part of the presenter to develop and rehearse this type of content, but the results are worth it.

The audience will either read your slides or listen to you. They will not do both. So, ask yourself this: is it more important that they listen, or more effective if they read?

Mark Templeton
CEO, Citrix

Case Study: Mark Templeton
Communication Pays Off

Mark Templeton credits his trajectory from mid-level manager to CEO solely to his personal investment in communication. Once a manager focused on tactics, he evolved into a leader by becoming a student of communications and learning how to instill vision.

Studying storytelling and leveraging his innate ability to think visually helped Templeton become a leader able to easily convey his vision for Citrix—a task not easily done given the abstract and invisible nature of the company's products and solutions. "My goal is to say more with fewer words," says Templeton, "and the presentation medium forces you to put all your thoughts into a consumable sequence."

Not that his staff cuts him any slack: "There's an ongoing wager among my staff about how far into a meeting we'll get before I pick up a marker and start drawing on the whiteboard," he says. "But ultimately the visual approach pays off."

His communication investment has paid off for Citrix investors, too: the company became one of the fastest software companies to reach $1 billion in annual revenue.

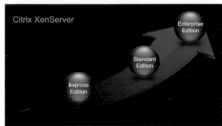

Part of what Templeton figured out early is that presentations should be simple and *support* his communication, not *be* his communication.

The Presentation Ecosystem

Jim Endicott, author of *The Presentation Survival Skills Guide,* refers to the presentation development process as a three-legged stool—message, visual story, and delivery.

As a presenter, you rely on the interdependence of your ideas, graphics, and execution. As an audience member, how many times have you attended a presentation only to wonder, after it's too late to extricate yourself gracefully, why you're there? The presenter may be very well-prepared and as fired up as a televangelist, but it's impossible to figure out the intent and why it's worth caring about. Most likely, the presenter focused on their "message" leg—dumping everything they know onto individual slides—but forgot to give equal attention to developing the "visual story" and "delivery" legs of the stool.

Presenters often read their slides instead of putting in the effort necessary to transform them into visual stories that support their message.

Today's presentation graphics tend to distract audiences. The result might be described as visual vertigo: audiences are jarred by having to resolve graphical disparities and dissonances that arise from poorly rendered perspectives, inconsistent lighting sources, and exasperating animations. Whether or not the content and delivery are good, people exposed to crudely constructed media will walk away from a presentation subtly agitated and thus less receptive to the message. Even worse, visuals devoid of clarity can cause a subliminal lack of trust. The presenter doesn't realize that the audience members care solely about what the presenter can do for them.

You also need to better anticipate the audience's needs initially and adjust the delivery accordingly. Presentations are quickly moving from face-to-face to exponentially more powerful mass media. How many times have you developed a presentation with the sole intent of delivering it in-person—only to find out later that a much larger audience will view it online? You'll need to modify that same content so that it resonates with its web-based audience.

This is a sensitive ecosystem. Striking a harmonious balance is important. Odds are high that you've been on both sides of the podium. As presenters, the natural tendency is to stay in your own zone, thinking more about how successful you'll feel instead of how your content, visuals, and delivery will be perceived.

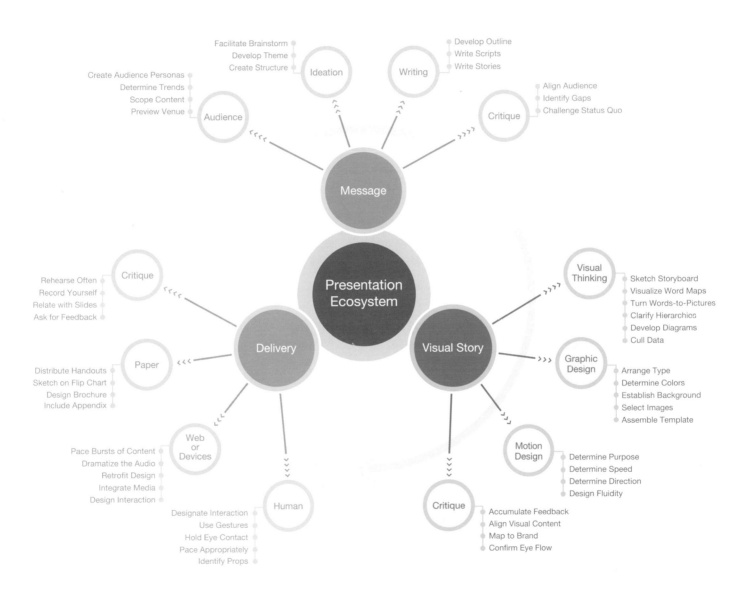

Facilitate Brainstorm
Develop Theme
Create Structure

Ideation

Writing

Develop Outline
Write Scripts
Write Stories

Create Audience Personas
Determine Trends
Scope Content
Preview Venue

Audience

Critique

Align Audience
Identify Gaps
Challenge Status Quo

Message

Presentation Ecosystem

Rehearse Often
Record Yourself
Relate with Slides
Ask for Feedback

Critique

Visual Thinking

Sketch Storyboard
Visualize Word Maps
Turn Words-to-Pictures
Clarify Hierarchies
Develop Diagrams
Cull Data

Delivery

Visual Story

Distribute Handouts
Sketch on Flip Chart
Design Brochure
Include Appendix

Paper

Graphic Design

Arrange Type
Determine Colors
Establish Background
Select Images
Assemble Template

Pace Bursts of Content
Dramatize the Audio
Retrofit Design
Integrate Media
Design Interaction

Web or Devices

Motion Design

Determine Purpose
Determine Speed
Determine Direction
Design Fluidity

Designate Interaction
Use Gestures
Hold Eye Contact
Pace Appropriately
Identify Props

Human

Critique

Accumulate Feedback
Align Visual Content
Map to Brand
Confirm Eye Flow

World Class Presentations Require Time and Focus

It's easy to get impatient with the creative process, but investing enough time is critical to developing a great presentation. Though time is often one's most valuable resource, there's no way to avoid spending it if you want a powerful and persuasive speech. Additionally, though the creative process can be messy and involve more iterations than you ever imagined, keep in mind that exploration, informal input, and review cycles ultimately lead to a stronger result.

The amount of time required to develop a presentation is directly proportional to how high the stakes are.

Sometimes recycling an old keynote with minimal modification works. Other times, when there's a big deal to close or a critical vision to present, you need to start from scratch and follow a creative process that takes into account both audience needs and feedback from colleagues.

Recently, during a Q&A session about presentations, someone asked, "I was up until 2 a.m. this morning building a presentation to deliver today. What am I doing wrong?" When asked when he started, the answer was predictable: "Yesterday afternoon." Clearly, the presentation was of low priority, or the employee seriously misjudged the time required. Either way, there's little doubt that the presentation could have benefited from better planning.

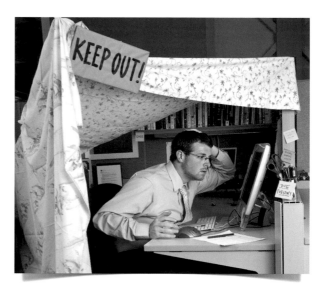

Once you know you have a speaking engagement, immediately schedule preparation time and review cycles on your calendar.

Below are some average timeframes and steps for an hour-long presentation that has 30 slides.

Time Estimate for Developing a Presentation

6–20 hours
Research and collect input from the web, colleagues, and the industry.

1 hour
Build an audience-needs map.

2 hours
Generate ideas via sticky notes.

1 hour
Organize the ideas.

1 hour
Have colleagues critique or collaborate around the impact the ideas will have on audience.

2 hours
Sketch a structure and/or a storyboard.

20–60 hours
Build the slides in a presentation application.

3 hours
Rehearse, rehearse, rehearse (in the shower, on the treadmill, or during the commute)

36–90 hours total

Responding to Audience Needs

Before beginning a presentation, it's important to ask yourself questions about your audience. Who are they? What are their needs, and how can you address them? How can the information you have make their lives better? What do you want them to do after the presentation is over? Questions like these are critical to developing relevant, resonant content.

Thinking about the audience will ensure you are placing their needs first, and give you a benchmark against which you can check your message.

Describe your audience, including some combination of their fears and needs, and state the opportunities and challenges you need to address in your communications. And of course, don't overlook their state of mind when they sit down to hear your message.

Most importantly, share the benefits of your position and provide the audience something to do after the presentation—a call to action. Whether your presentation goal is to share information or recruit people to a cause, you are faced with the same challenge of getting the audience to follow through. What should they do with the information you've provided them? You can relay your message time and time again, but the audience can't act on the message until you tell them what's in it for them.

Those with the most to lose—and the most to gain—are the listeners. Define their needs, surpass their expectations, and turn them into agents of your cause. Without your audience, you are nothing.

Consider the kind of relationship you want to have with your audience. Do you want to be their hero? Their mentor? Their cheerleader? Like these characters, good presenters aren't in it for themselves; they're in it for others. Take note.

Consider this list of questions when trying to understand an audience. Remember, presentations and audiences may vary, but one important fact remains constant: the audience didn't come to see you; they came to see what you can do for them.

Seven Questions to Knowing Your Audience

① What are they like?
Demographics and psychographics are a great start, but connecting with your audience means understanding them on a personal level. Take a walk in their shoes and describe what their life looks like.

② Why are they here?
What do they think they're going to get out of this presentation? Why did they come to hear you? Are they willing participants or mandatory attendees? This is also a bit of a situation analysis.

③ What keeps them up at night?
Everyone has a fear, a pain point, a thorn in the side. Let your audience know you empathize—and offer a solution.

④ How can you solve their problem?
What's in it for the audience? How are you going to make their lives better?

⑤ What do you want them to do?
Answer the question "so what?" Make sure there's clear action for your audience to take.

⑥ How might they resist?
What will keep them from adopting your message and carrying out your call to action?

⑦ How can you best reach them?
People vary in how they prefer to receive information. This can include everything from the setup of the room to the availability of materials after the presentation. Give the audience what they want, how they want it.

WWW

To ensure you keep your audience needs top-of-mind, download an audience persona slide.

How Do You Define Your Audience?

Here's an example. Most of the success of a presentation stems from how well it resonates with its audience—and audiences are many and diverse. Some messages have to reach people of all ages, across the economic spectrum, of all beliefs and backgrounds. Other messages have a very narrow target audience that can be distinctly defined. Reaching the audience doesn't happen by accident; it happens from respecting audiences' various needs, concerns, and fears; by talking to them in a way that builds trust and establishes emotional connections; by anticipating questions, or even resistance; and by providing a call to action.

How can you leverage this insight in your own presentations? Start by building audience personas before building slides. Painting a picture of a real human with real needs helps you connect to them more effectively.

Place an audience persona slide at the beginning of your deck; this way you can refer back to the people you're trying to reach. First, find or draw an image that represents a typical audience member or two. You can even give them names if it helps you feel like they are real. Then answer all the questions from the previous page and put it all on one slide. The slide is for you as context as you build your file, and shouldn't be projected.

This process helps build a scenario of what their life looks like. You need to figure out what motivates them.

The next page provides an example of what this persona might look like. In this case, you're profiling a couple—Ken and Kerry, baby boomers who are planning to attend a seminar about investments. This is a single persona; as a presenter, you should create as many profiles as the diversity of your audience warrants.

After preparing this persona, the presenter can draw these inferences and make these three critical points in the presentation:

There's no need for compromise: they can plan for a secure retirement without having to give up the good life.

There's minimal financial risk: limited upfront investment, competitive interest rates, and easy transfer of ownership work in the buyers' favor.

There are rewards for helping spread the word: exposing others in the peer group to properties designed for their specific lifestyle is easy and has significant benefits.

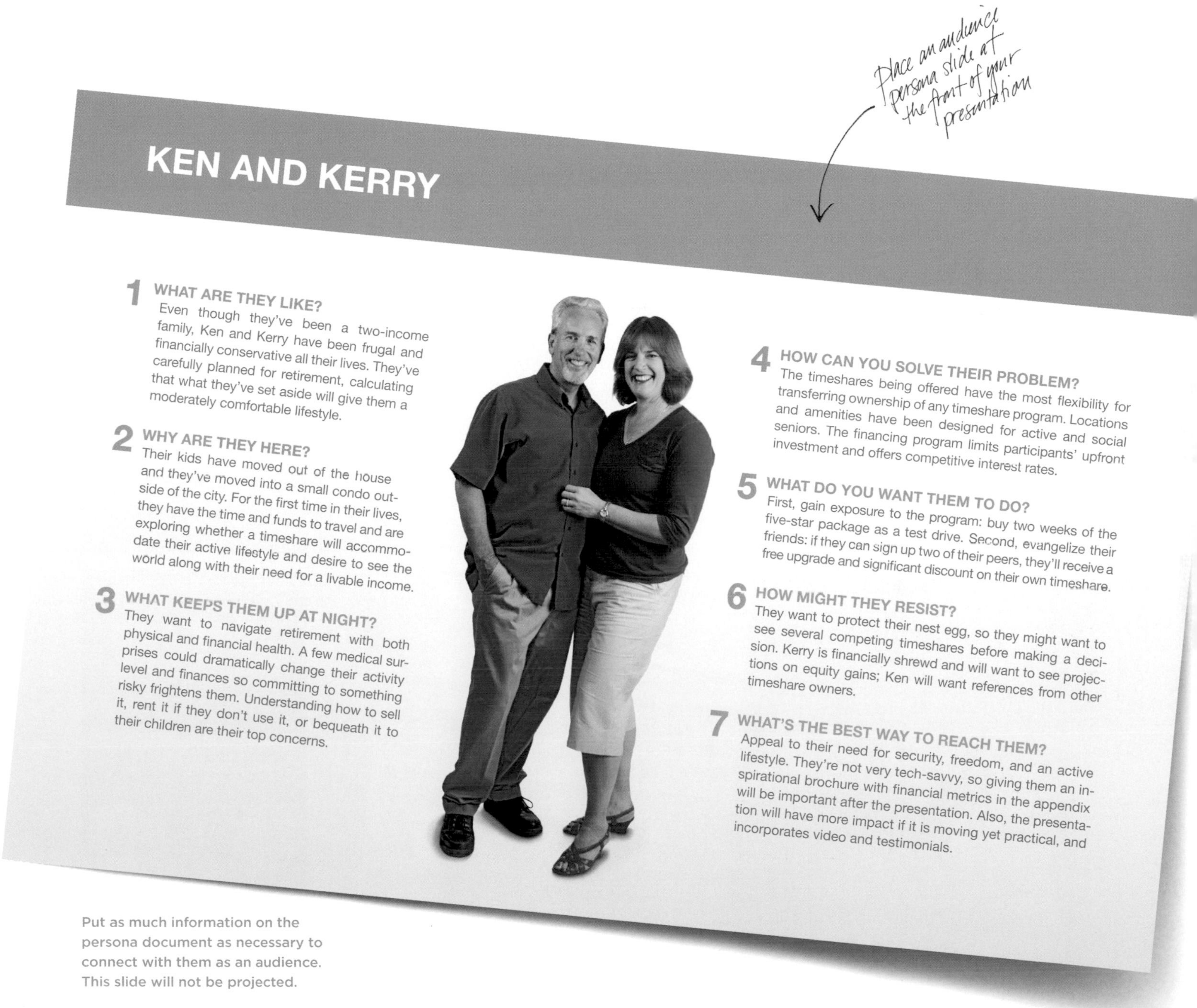
Place an audience persona slide at the front of your presentation
KEN AND KERRY
1 WHAT ARE THEY LIKE?
Even though they've been a two-income family, Ken and Kerry have been frugal and financially conservative all their lives. They've carefully planned for retirement, calculating that what they've set aside will give them a moderately comfortable lifestyle.
2 WHY ARE THEY HERE?
Their kids have moved out of the house and they've moved into a small condo outside of the city. For the first time in their lives, they have the time and funds to travel and are exploring whether a timeshare will accommodate their active lifestyle and desire to see the world along with their need for a livable income.
3 WHAT KEEPS THEM UP AT NIGHT?
They want to navigate retirement with both physical and financial health. A few medical surprises could dramatically change their activity level and finances so committing to something risky frightens them. Understanding how to sell it, rent it if they don't use it, or bequeath it to their children are their top concerns.
4 HOW CAN YOU SOLVE THEIR PROBLEM?
The timeshares being offered have the most flexibility for transferring ownership of any timeshare program. Locations and amenities have been designed for active and social seniors. The financing program limits participants' upfront investment and offers competitive interest rates.
5 WHAT DO YOU WANT THEM TO DO?
First, gain exposure to the program: buy two weeks of the five-star package as a test drive. Second, evangelize their friends: if they can sign up two of their peers, they'll receive a free upgrade and significant discount on their own timeshare.
6 HOW MIGHT THEY RESIST?
They want to protect their nest egg, so they might want to see several competing timeshares before making a decision. Kerry is financially shrewd and will want to see projections on equity gains; Ken will want references from other timeshare owners.
7 WHAT'S THE BEST WAY TO REACH THEM?
Appeal to their need for security, freedom, and an active lifestyle. They're not very tech-savvy, so giving them an inspirational brochure with financial metrics in the appendix will be important after the presentation. Also, the presentation will have more impact if it is moving yet practical, and incorporates video and testimonials.

Put as much information on the persona document as necessary to connect with them as an audience. This slide will not be projected.

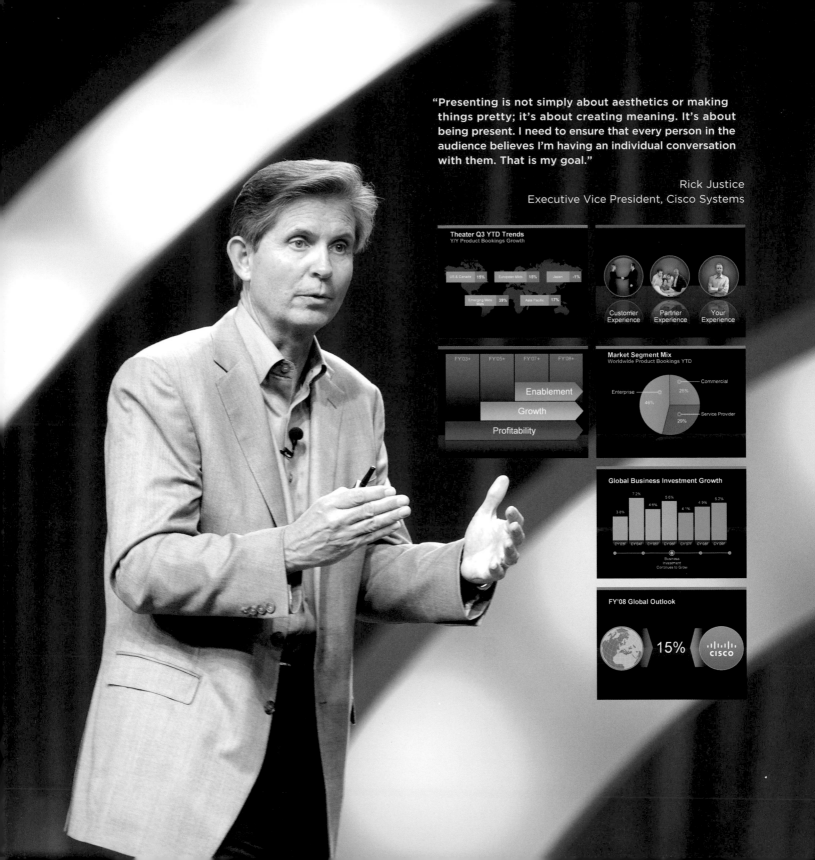

Case Study: Rick Justice
Creating Great Presence

Too often, presenters assume they'll be successful based on their stage presence alone. What they usually underestimate is the importance of the story they're about to tell—a story that is developed in a time-intensive, collaborative process that requires considering one's message, becoming intimate with the content and staging, and rehearsing, rehearsing, rehearsing.

One of those presenters who understands this principle is Rick Justice, Executive Vice President of Cisco. For his presentations, Justice pulls together a team of business, strategy, and communications experts. He sets the tone for a collaborative environment where all ideas are encouraged. The first brainstorm is always about context: What is the setting of the presentation? Who are the members of the audience? What messages do they need to hear from Cisco's executive team? What's the call to action? Once the context is determined, the team works to develop a storyline and message.

Justice's story development team works in a presentation command center decked out with all the latest technology, including Cisco's TelePresence, a digital whiteboard and multiple screens for the many collaborators using laptops.

His gutsy approach centers on trying innovative new ideas and employing technologies that communicate his message in a way that resonates with the audience.

"In most cases," says Justice, "I've got a few thousand people in the audience and just one chance to capture their imaginations by showing them something they've never seen before while ensuring the content is relevant and inspiring to them."

As ideas are collected, the presentation team organizes them in a blocking document. During meetings, this meta structure is displayed at all times—and tweaked on an ongoing basis—so the team can stay focused on the big ideas while completing all supporting detailed content. Justice explains, "If we focus too early on perfecting a single idea, we'll lose the chance to explore other, potentially better ideas as we go through the story development process."

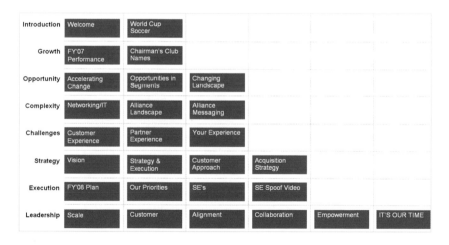

Introduction	Welcome	World Cup Soccer				
Growth	FY'07 Performance	Chairman's Club Names				
Opportunity	Accelerating Change	Opportunities in Segments	Changing Landscape			
Complexity	Networking/IT	Alliance Landscape	Alliance Messaging			
Challenges	Customer Experience	Partner Experience	Your Experience			
Strategy	Vision	Strategy & Execution	Customer Approach	Acquisition Strategy		
Execution	FY'08 Plan	Our Priorities	SE's	SE Spoof Video		
Leadership	Scale	Customer	Alignment	Collaboration	Empowerment	IT'S OUR TIME

Case Study: ZS Associates
An Incentive to Communicate Clearly

When consulting firm ZS Associates wanted a presentation to relaunch their incentive compensation solution, they needed to convey both the firm's market dominance and their application's ease of use. The original visual story attempted to communicate too much information and, as a result, didn't convey how easy the solution is to use.

To distill their presentation, the first step was creating a new story from their existing presentation. Their slides contained important information that could be included in a new script.

BEFORE (example 1a)

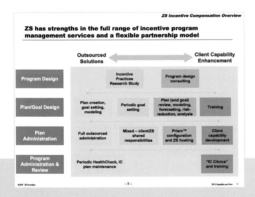

BEFORE (example 1b)

Rather than just clean up the original slides, the content was conceptually reorganized. By thinking outside the slide and focusing on the message, it became apparent that what was thought to be a three-prong service strategy was in reality four. The two slides were replaced with a visual overview of the services.

AFTER (example 1)

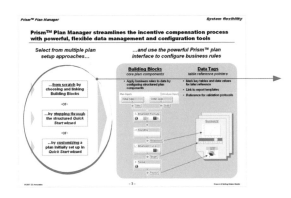

BEFORE (example 2)

In the original slide the technical details on the right half of the slide distracted from the message. The main message was that there are three easy ways to install Javelin. To avoid confusion, it's better to split the content across more than one slide.

AFTER (example 2)

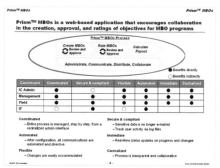

BEFORE (example 3a)

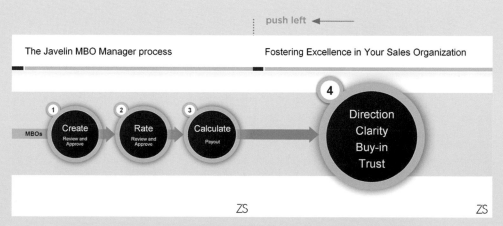

BEFORE (example 3b)

Many MBO (Management by Objectives) programs are complex, and ZS Software cuts through the complexity.

The content circled in orange was the only part addressed verbally. So reducing the amount of additional information and using a series of slides to show the impact of an effective MBO program highlights the effectiveness and simplicity of the ZS solution.

If your message is "simplicity," then your slides should feel simple.

Most presentation applications have a push transition. When applied, the entire slide exits the screen as the next slide enters. It creates the sense of a larger space.

AFTER (example 3a)

AFTER (example 3b)

People participating in these programs can feel frustrated, and the product was built specifically to address those issues.

To give a human face to the new software, the presentation used stylized, full-bleed photos combined with quotes of common frustrations, now resolved. These slides introduced each section of the presentation.

"I sleep better knowing that my incentive program is working and my reps are happy."

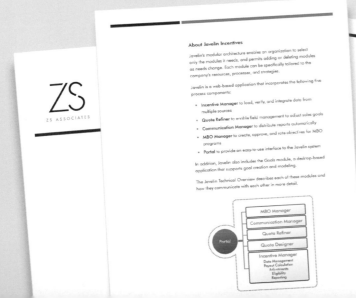

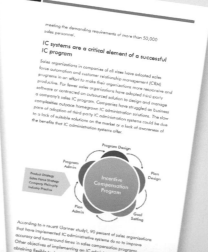

Instead of printing out the presentation as-is, the audience received a handout that incorporated infographics from the presentation.

CHAPTER 2

Creating Ideas, Not Slides

Finding Your Inspiration

Much of communication today has the quality of intangibility. Services, software, causes, thought leadership, change management, company vision—they're often more conceptual than concrete, more ephemeral than firm. And there's nothing wrong with that. But it's a struggle communicating these types of ideas because essentially they are invisible. It's difficult to share one's vision when there's nothing to see.

Expressing these invisible ideas visually, so that they feel tangible and can be acted upon, is a bit of an art form. The best place to start is not with the computer. A pencil and a sheet of paper will do nicely.

Why take this seemingly Luddite approach? Because presentation software was never intended to be a brainstorming or drawing tool.

The applications are simply containers for ideas and assets, not the means to generate them.

It's been an easy trap to fall into, launching presentation applications to prepare content. In reality, the best creative process requires stepping away from technology and relying on the same tools of expression that you grew up with—pens, pencils, and crayons. The goal is to generate ideas—not necessarily pictures yet—*but lots of ideas*. These can be words, diagrams, or scenes; they can be literal or metaphorical; the only requirement is that they express your underlying thoughts. The best thing about this process is that you don't need to figure out how to use drawing tools or where to save the file. Everything you need you already have (and don't say you can't draw; you're just out of practice). This means you can generate a large quantity of ideas in a relatively short amount of time. And that's your primary objective when generating ideas: to create a large quantity of them.

And you wondered where all Dali's liquid inspiration came from

Change your environment when you need to be creative. Find a spot away from your desk. Yeah, Salvador Dali was a bit eccentric, but try writing your next speech in the tub with paper and pencil and just see if it's not better.

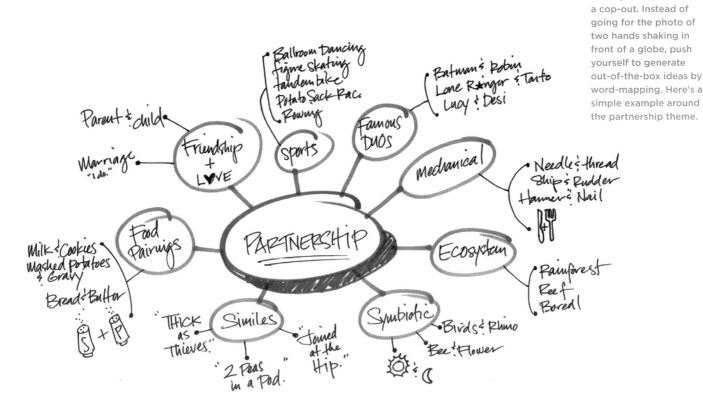

Cheesy metaphors are a cop-out. Instead of going for the photo of two hands shaking in front of a globe, push yourself to generate out-of-the-box ideas by word-mapping. Here's a simple example around the partnership theme.

Often ideas come immediately. That's good, but avoid the potential pitfall of going with the first thing that comes to mind.

Continue to sketch and force yourself to think through several more ideas. It takes discipline and tenacity—especially when it feels like you solved it on the first try. Explore words and word associations to generate several ideas. Use word-mapping techniques, where you write or draw word associations like in the example above. Digital natives might prefer mind-mapping software for this phase. Stronger solutions frequently appear after four or five ideas have percolated to the top. Continue generating ideas even if they seem to wander down unrelated paths. You never know what you might find, after all.

Once you've generated an enormous amount of ideas, identify a handful that meet the objective of the vision or concept you're trying to communicate. It matters less what form they take at this point than that they get your message across.

Take the time and spend the creative energy because the payoff will be a presentation that people not only remember, but one that inspires them to action.

Innovating with Sticky Notes

Great inventions combine new technology with widespread applicability. In the case of the Post-It, a scientist at 3M applied low tack adhesive to paper and used it to mark his hymnal for choir practice at church. That's how this favorite brainstorm medium was born.

Sticky notes allow ideas to be captured, sorted, and re-arranged as needed.

When generating ideas, one idea per sticky note is preferable. And use a Sharpie. The reason? If it takes more space than a Post-It and requires more detail than a Sharpie can provide, the idea is too complex.

Simplicity is the essence of clear communication. Additionally, sticky notes make it easy to re-order content until the structure and flow feel right. On the other hand, many people prefer a more traditional storyboarding approach, preferring to linearly articulate detailed ideas. That's fine, too. The point is not to prescribe exactly how to work, but to encourage you to generate a lot of ideas and to do so quickly.

For other ideas in content development methodologies, check out Decker Communication's grid at www.decker.com and Cliff Atkinson's *Beyond Bullet Points* at www.beyondbullets.com.

T!P
When brainstorming, don't settle for the first solution. Think through multiple alternatives. Don't be stingy with the sticky notes.

Whatever your brainstorming method, remember the following guidelines:

Rule #1:
POSTPONE & WITHHOLD your judgment of !IDEAS

Rule #2:
ENCOURAGE WILD EXAGGERATED ideas

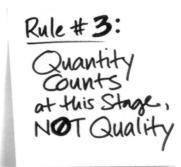

Rule #3:
Quantity Counts at this Stage, NOT Quality

Rule #4:
BUILD ON IDEAS put forward BY OTHERS

Rule #5:
every person & every IDEA has = worth

After you've created an enormous amount of ideas, classify them, challenge them, and filter them down to a core set of meaningful ideas that will resonate.

Case Study: Bill McDonough
Sketching Live

Bill McDonough likes to draw on screen in front of his audience because it offers him the chance to interact with his content.

Like a professor on his blackboard, McDonough often hits the B key while in slide show mode to make his slide a blank slate on which he can project sketches from his pen tablet. He believes that the audience should process charts one point at a time instead of all at once. Many of his charts are drawn by hand. Complex charts can be obscure or the point may not be evident, so McDonough draws the charts as he speaks to amplify the hidden points.

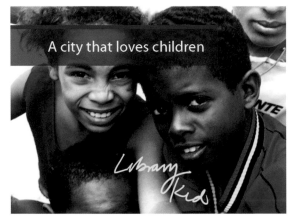

One of the great moments of education for McDonough was when he was with the Chancellor of Vanderbilt University at a Rotary Club lunch. The Chancellor stood up and said, "What is it about education in America, that you walk into a room full of six-year-olds and say, 'How many people here can draw?' and every hand goes up, 'I can draw. I can draw anything.' And then you walk into a classroom full of graduate students and you say, 'How many people here can draw?' and almost no one thinks they can. What kind of an education system is this?"

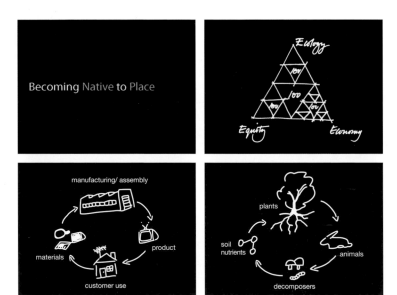

"I think drawing is a celebration and connection to my childhood. To draw in public is to open yourself to people with a kind of innocence and hope. Sketching adds interest to the presentation and if you mess up, it's just a human act and people forgive your scribbles."

Bill McDonough
Author and founder of
William McDonough + Partners

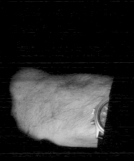

Sketching Your Way to Success

Sketching is the magical part of the process—taking rough ideas, fine tuning them, re-organizing them, and sketching it out all over again until you can see a story.

Storyboarding can be intimidating. Here's how Dave Gray, founder of XPLANE, teaches the art of drawing stick figures.

1 Most people start a stick figure by drawing the head. This is a mistake. Because a stick figure represents a whole person, the best way to draw one should reflect the way you see a whole person. Think about what you notice first when seeing someone from a distance. It's nearly always the body—the center of gravity and motion. Starting with the body allows you to capture the essence of the gesture you want to convey.

2 After you've drawn the body in the position that you want, draw in a circle for the head. The placement of the head in relation to the body is essential. Happiness, angst, speed and sluggishness are all conveyed by the relative positions of the head and body. Observe people doing their daily routines and you'll see it for yourself.

3 Next, draw the facial expression. Your basic smiley face or frowny face will work just fine. Adding a little angle for a nose will help show which direction the head is pointing. This can be especially important when you want to show two people interacting with each other.

4 Add the legs next—they are more essential to conveying gesture than the arms. The primary energy that propels a basketball comes not from your arms but from your legs (watch basketball on TV and you can actually see this). The energy of a stick figure works the same way. Use small ovals to represent feet; this helps ground your character.

5 Now, draw the arms and complete the gesture you started with the legs.

T!P
Go to a public place and see if you can capture the gestures of the people around you in stick figure drawings. This is a great way to hone your observation skills.

Don't worry about the quality of your sketches. Above are three sketches of mine that depict different aspects of the process of having lunch. All relay the same idea, yet they're distinctly different. The first sketch was the most obvious, but when given more thought, additional—and potentially better—ideas appear.

Collaborating to Get Clarity

Often, ideas that seem clear and straightforward in one's own head can be confounding to others. That's why it's important to explore multiple ways of visualizing an idea. Don't rely solely on words to get your point across either; make sketches of what you see when you are speaking.

Then, bring in a colleague or two and walk them through the sketches. Ask them to listen not only to your words but to evaluate whether or not the sketches capture your intent. If they become confused while you are talking, have them ask clarifying questions or sketch out their own version of your ideas.

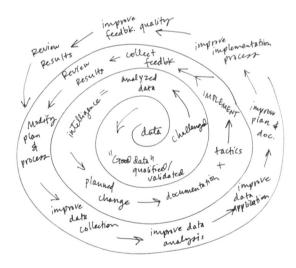

WHAT HE SAID
In visualizing his ideas, one executive sketched this diagram. It reads as a spiral or a single, linear flow.

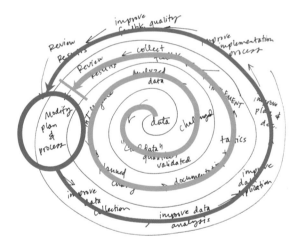

WHAT HE MEANT
After considering the executive's intent, two types of flow emerged: the process begins as a linear sequence from the center, but at the point he got to "modify, plan, and process" it turns into a circular flow.

■ Occurs once in process
■ Continues in a cycle

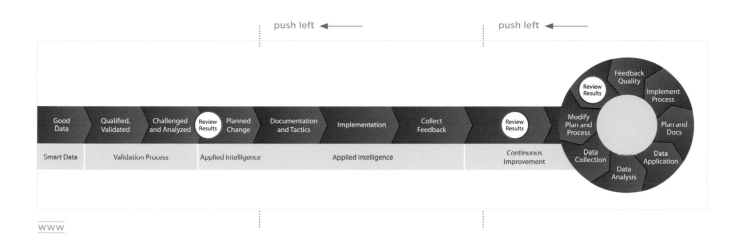

push left ←

push left ←

| Good Data | Qualified, Validated | Challenged and Analyzed | Review Results | Planned Change | Documentation and Tactics | Implementation | Collect Feedback | | Review Results | Modify Plan and Process | Review Results | Feedback Quality | Implement Process | Plan and Docs | Data Application |

Smart Data — Validation Process — Applied Intelligence — Applied Intelligence — Continuous Improvement — Data Collection — Data Analysis

www

WHAT THE DESIGNER CREATED
The flow splits over a series of three slides. Using a push transition, it reveals the multi-faceted process. The content from the green line on the left is a linear flow occurring in the first two slides above. The third slide relates to the orange line and is expressed as a circular flow. Splitting the content across three slides made it legible and ensured that each phase of the process received the proper focus.

T!P
It's important to test drive your presentation with colleagues before taking it out on the road.

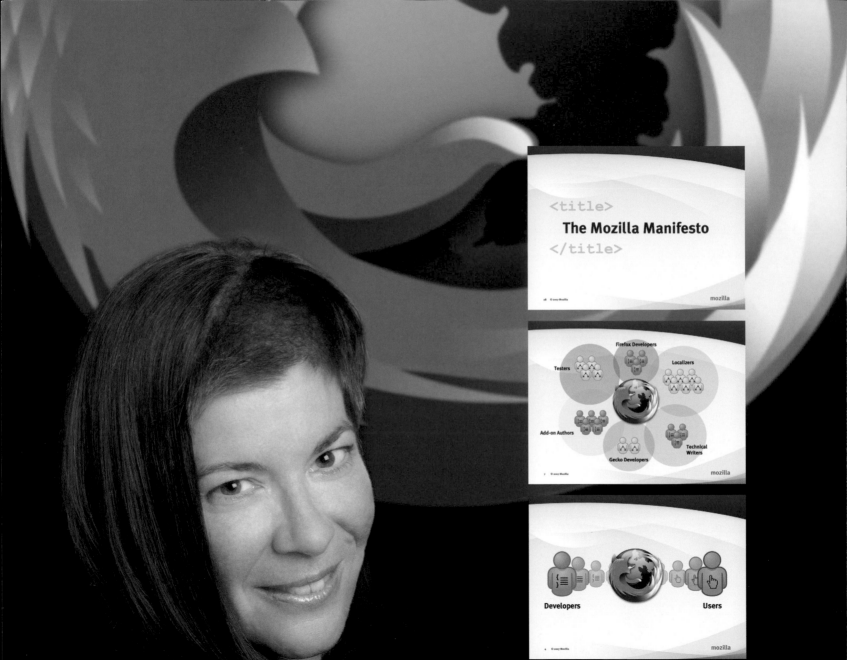

Case Study: Mitchell Baker
Using Images Worth a Thousand Words

The old saying about the value of a picture was written even prior to globalization. Today, in the increasingly multilingual world, it's dangerous to assume that English language messages will always hit the mark. It's become more necessary than ever to present our ideas via a universal medium.

Perhaps there's no better example of this than Mitchell Baker's keynote at CeBIT Australia. As CEO of open-source pioneer Mozilla, she needed to connect with more than 3,000 attendees from more than a dozen countries by making sure her vision didn't get lost in translation.

For this conference, the imagery served as the mechanism for the message, allowing Mitchell to tell her story the way she wanted, and it translated across languages and cultures.

Strategies for Cross-culture Communication

1. Use images that are culturally neutral. Images translate, words don't. Instead of using slides loaded with bullets, experiment with a visual approach.

2. Keep graphics extremely simple. Not all cultures process info from left to right. Simplifying is essential. You could animate the content so it gradually appears—guiding the order the audience should process it.

3. Connect with your audience. Detailed scripts actually hinder presenters from making that connection. Slides should provide a structure for presenters without cramping their style or putting words in their mouths.

In the end, a great presentation should transcend linguistic, geographic, and cultural boundaries. Truth is truth.

Sketching Ideas Using Diagrams

When transforming your words to images, create loose sketches of several ideas for each concept. In this example, shapes and relationships are important, but so is the inclusion of a human form. The reason? The presenter needed to convey that to manage the software development process, one must also manage people's processes.

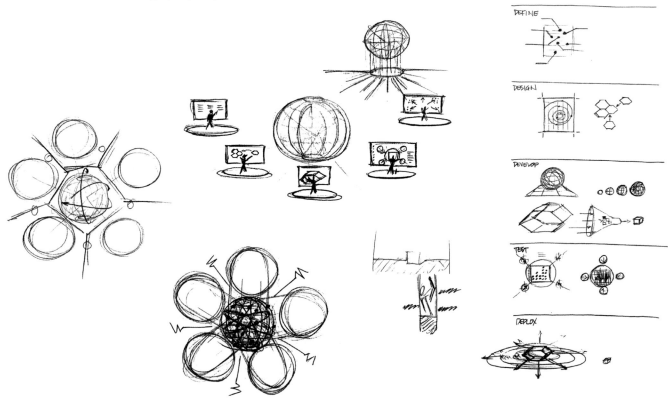

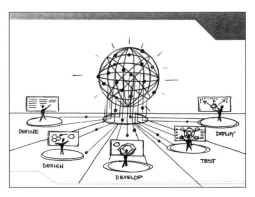

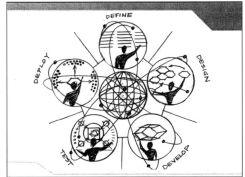

Both these sketches convey the same concept. The first one was eliminated because it over-glorified the management system instead of focusing on the way developers work.

The Orchestration

Architect

Analyst

Manage

Developer

Operations

Tester

You Are Not Alone

Design

Define

Manage

Develop

Deploy

Test

Photos of various employees add the human element. In the first sequence, they take turns looking at each other to show they can communicate through a managed system. The second scene depicts them working at their respective tasks while remaining connected via the management function of the development environment.

Sketching Complete Ideas

Now that you've generated several ideas, begin to sketch pictures or scenes from them. These sketches become visual triggers that spark more ideas.

The sketching process should be loose and quick—doodles really. Search through stock houses, magazines, even YouTube for images and vignettes to reference while sketching. Generate as many pictures as you can while keeping in mind the slide layout; you want to ensure that the elements work spatially in that format. In this way, sketching serves as proof-of-concept because ideas that are too complex, time-consuming, or costly will present themselves as ripe for elimination.

Don't worry about throwing things away—that's why you generated a lot of ideas in the first place. In fact, you're ultimately going to have to throw all of them away except for one. Designers recognize this as the destructive aspect of the creative process; it's a good thing.

Some of the ideas you generate may require multiple scenes built across a few slides versus a snapshot on a single slide. On the other hand, sometimes it's as simple as using the perfect picture or diagram. Getting your great idea across might require that you manipulate an image, create a custom illustration, or produce a short video. Focus on whatever works best, not on the idea that's easiest to execute.

If you sketch, it can sometimes be difficult for others to imagine your overall vision. Collecting images that represent the feeling of the final artwork often helps communicate your intent.

Script: The garden that is the internet can be a dangerous place, and you don't always know when <SNAP!> something bad is going to happen.

There are plenty of dangers out there, and it takes all you've got to keep safe.

Now, find a colleague or two and walk them through your sketches. Have them give you feedback on what works, given your audience and personal style. They'll likely have insights that will improve your idea.

Here's where it gets a bit more difficult. Depending on the concept you've identified as the one best suited to convey your idea, you may or may not have the skills to execute the idea digitally. Be prepared to enlist the help of a designer (you did plan far enough ahead to make sure you've got one available, right?). There's no shame in seeking professional help, after all; what's important is effective communication, regardless of whether you have the skill set to execute it.

T!P

Keep yourself visually and conceptually fed by watching films, visiting museums, and reading design-related publications.

But what if someone was looking out for you, taking care of menaces and eliminating threats before they become a problem?

That's what our virus stopper was designed to do—eliminate threats and protect your data so you can get back to business.

CHAPTER 3

Creating Diagrams

Classifying Diagrams

At my firm, we use sketchbooks to generate many ideas around a concept. I collected the sketchbooks of all the employees and created iconic representations of the most common diagrams. I cut these thousands of diagrams into little cards and sat on the floor for hours and sorted them. I felt like a little kid again.

After a long day hunched over the diagrams, a pattern and classification began to emerge. There were distinct differences in the diagrams and how they would be used to show relationships in information for professional communication.

A diagram is a good way to explain how parts of a whole interact. It's nearly impossible to communicate today without using shapes to symbolize various types of relationships and their interactions.

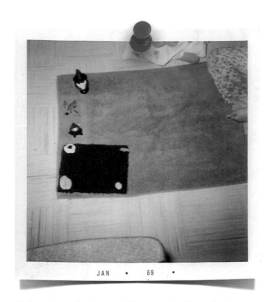

When I was little, I would sit on the floor for hours sorting and arranging objects, textures, and layers in a way that told a story.

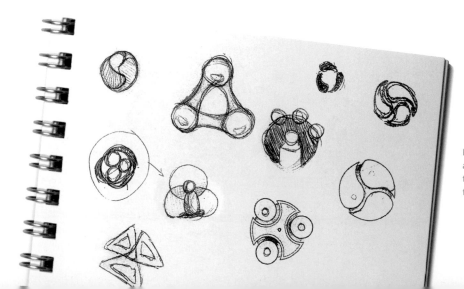

Relationships, patterns, and classifications of the diagrams emerged from the sketches.

The diagram section depicts examples of six common diagram types. The first four types show common shapes that can be used to explain various abstract relationships. The last two types show illustrated solutions of a more literal, realistic nature.

Below is a key for how the section is organized.

Abstract Concepts

Flow	Structure	Cluster	Radiate
Linear	Matrices	Overlapping	From a point
Circular	Trees	Closure	With a core
Divergent/Convergent	Layers	Enclosed	Without a core
Multidirectional		Linked	

Realistic Concepts

Pictorial	Display Data
Direction	Comparison
Location	Trend
Reveal	Distribution
Process	
Influence	

Abstract Concepts: Flow

Linear: Flow construction that illustrates a process with a definite start and end point. The diagram can follow a straight line or be a series of steps along a line.

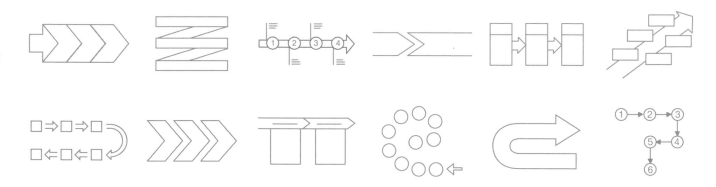

Circular: Flow that represents a continuous process without an end point. Any closed loop shape could work.

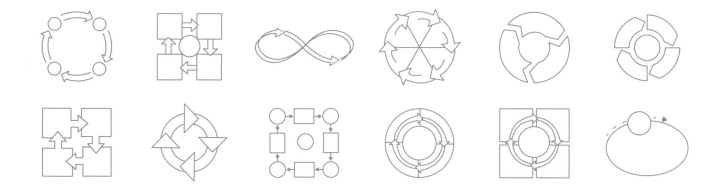

Divergent and Convergent: Flow that occurs when two or more elements either collide or separate out from each other as if splitting off.

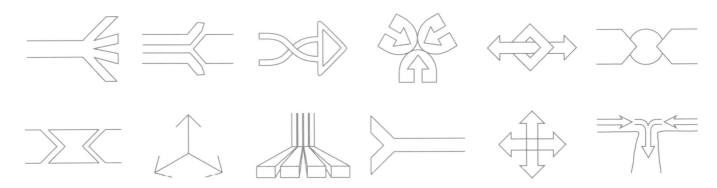

Multidirectional: Flow that expresses complex relationships—flow charts, for instance. Often these flows result from a combination of the preceding types.

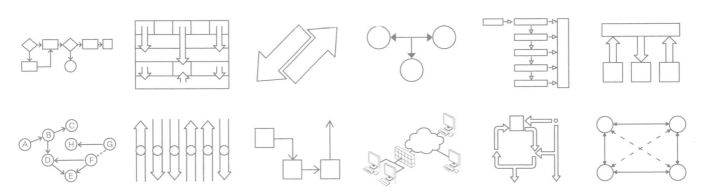

Abstract Concepts: Structure

Matrices: Structures that compare data with at least two different data sets. One set of data can even be a yes/no set of data, as in a checklist.

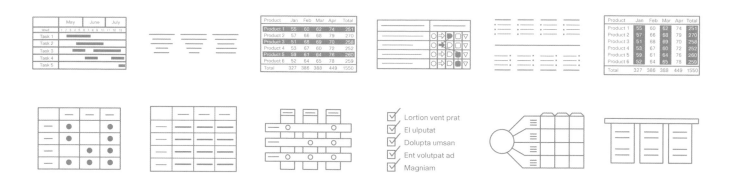

Trees: Structures that indicate clear hierarchy. Relationships can be expressed between any number of objects.

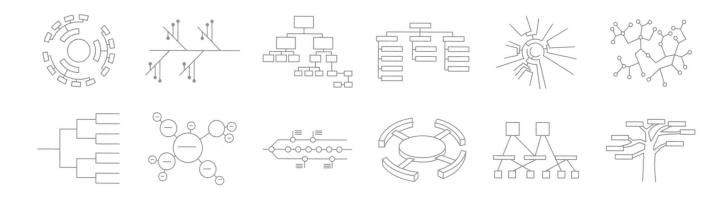

Layers: Structures that show elements that stack or build on each other. They can depict both hierarchy and sequence.

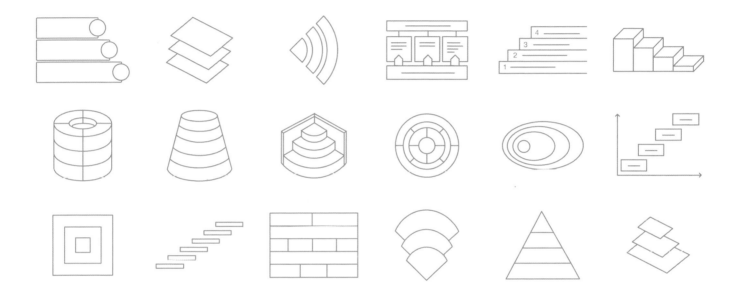

Abstract Concepts: Cluster

Overlapping: Clusters that overlap and indicate shared sets, interest, or responsibility. Sometimes they form a new shape or area within the overlap.

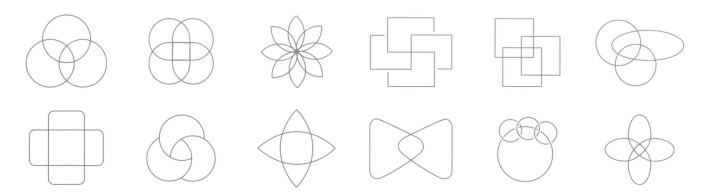

Closure: Clusters that emerge when shapes combine to create another shape. This principle of Gestalt psychology can be useful when expressing the idea that "the sum is greater than the parts."

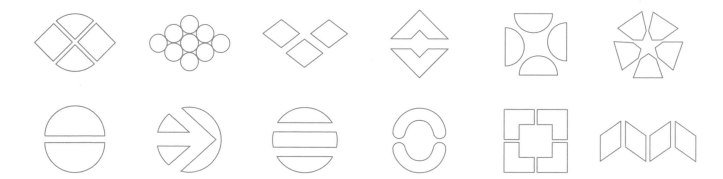

Enclosed: Clusters that are enclosed and contain at least one element that envelops another. Grouping in this way indicates which elements are part of a higher order, and which stand alone.

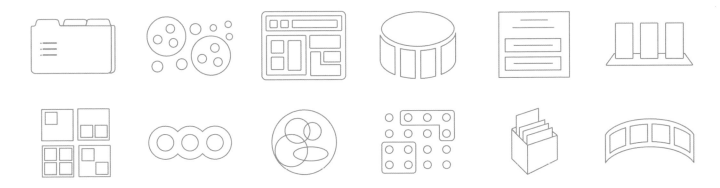

Linked: Clusters that are linked as a unifying element to group items. A unifying element links related groups of items. It could be a line, shape, or connector of any kind.

Abstract Concepts: Radiate

From a point: Occurs when a single directional "burst" emerges from either a graphic or point that has a clear point of origin.

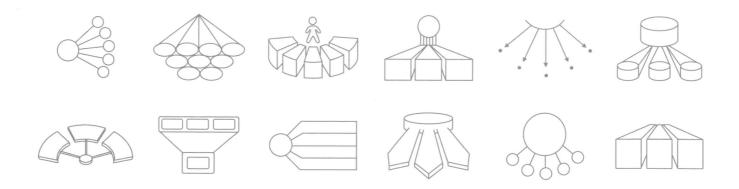

With a core: Creates a parent-child relationship. The outer elements connect with a central element to hold the family together.

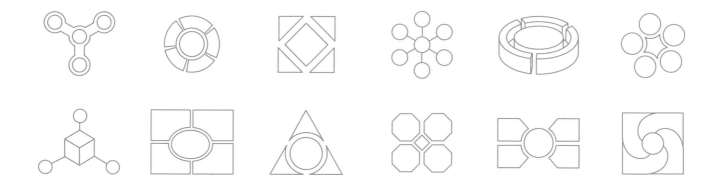

Without a core: Implies that elements connect through proximity or mutual attraction. They are tied to one central area.

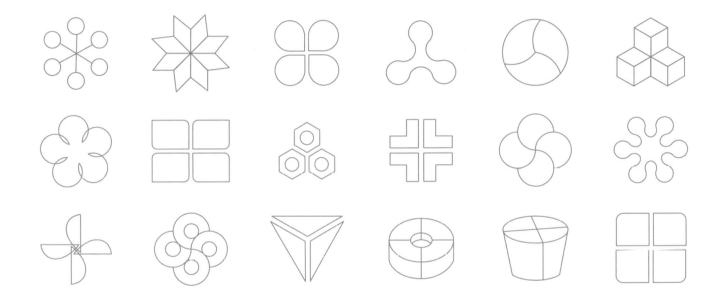

You've noticed that the abstract concepts are usually shapes that are combined to show relationships. In this next section you'll see a sampling of diagrams that are realistic. It is by no means exhaustive. There's no limit to how you tell your story visually.

Realistic Concepts: Pictorial

Process: A snapshot of how things work sequentially as a product or system.

 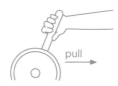   

Reveal: An illustration of hidden information shown by slicing, peeling, or otherwise exposing a thing's inner workings.

Direction: Showing where to go or how to get somewhere. They usually feature a starting location and destination, and may contain written directions.

Location: Showing where something is in the context of geography, topography, system, or shape. These diagrams call attention to a specific location while providing context.

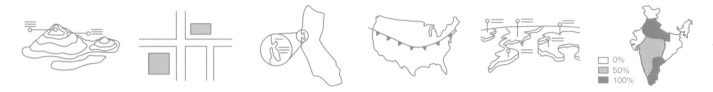

Influence: Demonstrating the resulting impact of various interacting elements.

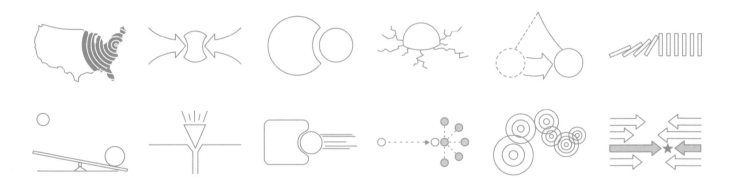

Realistic Concepts: Display Data

Comparison: Juxtaposition of two or more sets of information to illustrate differences. Bar graphs, pie charts, and any number of other methods are suitable.

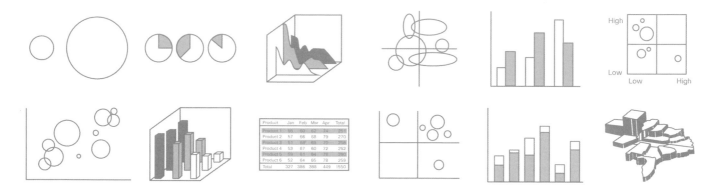

Trend: One parameter of the data represents time, to indicate a trend. Change over time is the most important aspect of these diagrams.

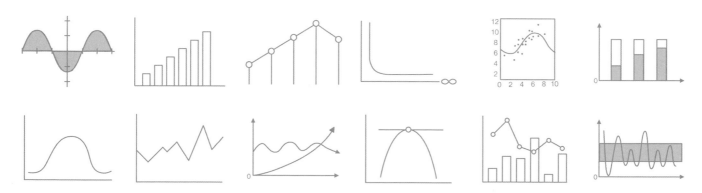

Distribution: Expression of a pattern in seemingly disparate data. Whether a scatter plot, bell curve, or other model, distribution diagrams correlate singular instances into a larger pattern.

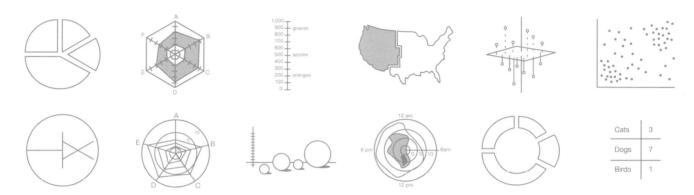

Including display data in the diagram section may seem illogical. But data displayed visually is a diagram of sorts—and it's often more clear when the display highlights the meaning of the information. Rather than oversimplify the complexities of statistics, successful information design can often incorporate multiple parameters, telling a richer story of cause-and-effect than data points alone.

Making Diagrams Work Together

Now that you've seen the building blocks for abstract and realistic concepts, you'll look at how to build them into a complex concept. Complex concepts can be communicated by connecting more than one diagram type. In the Silicon Valley, there are many presenters who need to explain software structures, web applications, and other invisible concepts visually. On the facing page is a concept sketch of a data warehouse solution that the customer called a "marketecture" diagram. It needed to show how the products and process work together like a "system."

A system similar to the one shown is a good way to represent elaborate and complex relationships. System diagrams can also show how things work or where things are. When presenting these complex relationships, remember that you want your audience to process one idea at a time—so this type of diagram needs to build over time.

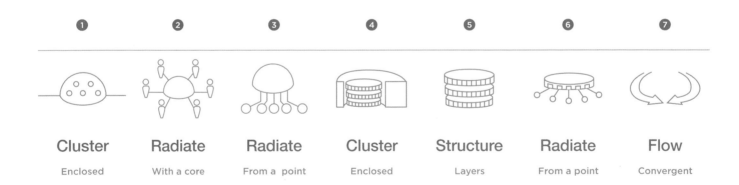

①	**②**	**③**	**④**	**⑤**	**⑥**	**⑦**
Cluster	**Radiate**	**Radiate**	**Cluster**	**Structure**	**Radiate**	**Flow**
Enclosed	With a core	From a point	Enclosed	Layers	From a point	Convergent

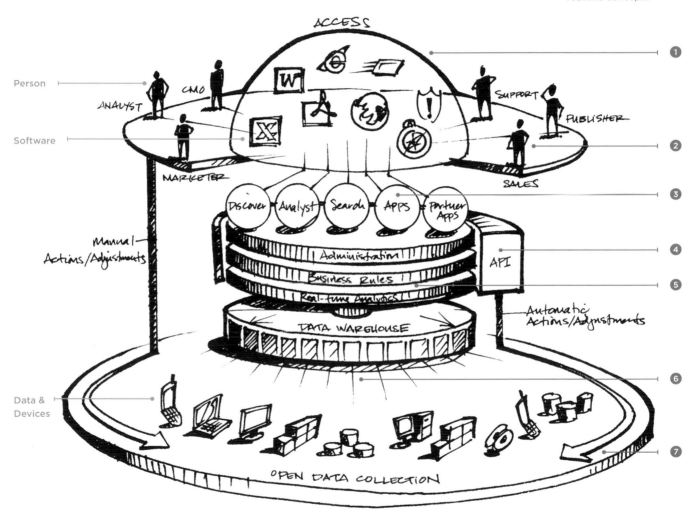

Here are the results of combining the seven abstract diagrams on the opposite page with realistic concepts.

1

2

3

4

5

6

7

ACCESS

Person

ANALYST

CMO

Software

MARKETER

SUPPORT

PUBLISHER

SALES

Discover   Analyst   Search   APPS   Partner APPS

Manual Actions/Adjustments

Administration

API

Business Rules

Real-time Analytics

Automatic Actions/Adjustments

DATA WAREHOUSE

Data & Devices

OPEN DATA COLLECTION

REALISTIC CONCEPTS

ABSTRACT CONCEPTS

Strengthening the Diagram's Concept

Taking more time to think through a concept can yield clearer meaning. Consider this example: the images on the left express concepts by means of simple diagrams. And they're fine. They work. To many people, these graphics are "good enough."

The concept is not as refined as it could have been. Rather, consider what occurs when the individual ideas are coalesced around a central character—the client. The target motif reinforced that advertisers can connect with a specific audience.

Suddenly, individual concepts become imbued with context, sequence, and association. In other words, a little bit of additional time and thought can go a long way.

BEFORE

IDEATE

AFTER

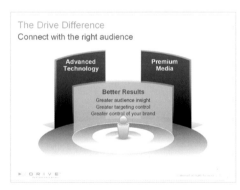

Nice graphics were used to create simple diagram concepts.

Sketches of various options: the company chose a solution that puts their client in the center.

Developed digitally, the new concepts behave as a strong set or family of graphics.

BEFORE   IDEATE   AFTER

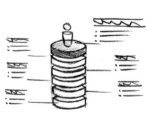

CHAPTER 4

Displaying Data

Following the Five Data Slide Rules

When it comes to displaying data in your presentation, you must adhere to one principle above all others: clarity.

Projecting your data on a slide puts you at an immediate disadvantage to printing it in a white paper or scientific text. In a presentation, the audience doesn't have the benefit of being able to pull your data in close to examine it.

So it is absolutely crucial that any data in your presentation carries with it a clear message. And you can keep that message clear by remembering this one fact:

Data slides are not really about the data. They are about the meaning of the data.

Most presenters don't really understand this distinction. How many times have you sat through presentations where the speaker referred to one complicated chart for five minutes, after which you still couldn't figure out the point of the slide?

The problem is that, most of the time, slides aren't a good medium for showing complex data. When it's important for your audience to examine the data and come to their own conclusions, you should distribute the data as a printout.

A cluttered or overwhelming data slide can derail even the most compelling speaker, so only show data in your presentation if the data helps you better illustrate your conclusions. And be sure to display it in a way that the audience can absorb easily (even from the cheap seats).

Use the following five principles to present your data in the clearest possible way:

---

1 Tell the truth

2 Get to the point

3 Pick the right tool for the job

4 Highlight what's important

5 Keep it simple

Telling the Truth

As a presenter, nothing commands like credibility. This is especially true when it comes to presenting data. Though it's unlikely that all the data can be clearly depicted on a single slide, successful presenters treat the data they do show with absolute integrity.

Additionally, be prepared to provide access to the complete data set, if requested, and be ready to answer questions about your conclusions.

Your audience deserves consideration here, too. Audiences that are analytical, scientific, or engineer-minded tend to look at data with a skeptical eye—it's what they're trained to do, after all. If your data has been boiled down or clarified too much, they may feel it has been manipulated, has become "marketing data," or is no longer substantial. To prevent these assumptions, avoid decorating your data; ornamentation can detract from credibility.

Expenses by Department

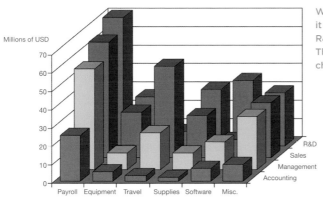

Millions of USD

Which graph makes it easier to determine R&D's travel expense? This 3D chart or the charts below?

2006 Expenses by Department in Millions of USD

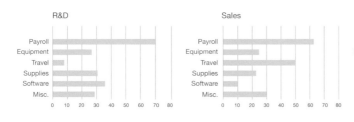

The charts above were provided by Stephen Few, author of *Show Me the Numbers* and *Information Dashboard Design*. He specializes in data visualization that increases comprehension. Both his books should be on your shelf along with everything Edward Tufte has written.

Getting to the Point

What is it you want your audience to "get" from your data? What's the message you want them to take away?

To communicate your data effectively, you first must articulate the conclusions you want your audience to adopt.

Begin by asking yourself, "What would I like them to remember about this data?" Usually, this will be a point about causality, such as the conditions that led to the results in your data, or the future conditions that the data most likely will create. Whatever the cause, you need to draw some kind of meaning from the data so that you can effectively express that meaning to your audience.

Consider the example below. At first glance one might conclude that the main point of the slide is that revenue has increased. Granted, that is a major point, but not the primary point that the presenter wanted the audience to walk away with. In reality, this presentation was delivered by the Human Resources department to petition an executive leadership team to give their department a larger budget. Just as sales had hit a low point in March, the HR department had rolled out a new sales training program. No other organizational changes had happened in that timeframe and they wanted to correlate the spike with their program. The most important information therefore was the point in time where their program was implemented.

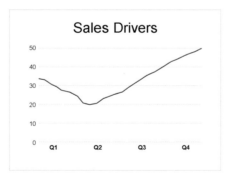

First impression on this chart is the enormous sales growth and recovery.

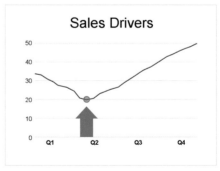

In reality, the purpose of this chart was for HR to draw attention to the March timeframe.

Once you are certain about the meaning of your data, you'll find it much easier to build the slide. Your conclusions will determine the type of graph you choose, and how (or if) you use emphasis.

These chart samples show that different types of conclusions can be drawn from the same data. Choosing what you want the audience to focus on is important so they process the information quickly.

This chart highlights Q1 to emphasize that this was the most successful quarter.

This chart emphasize that the Americas had the lowest revenue growth.

Here the focus is on when and where the revenue declined.

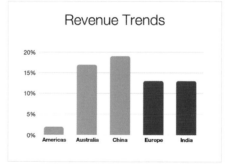

To show the total by region, it can stay in the context of the matrix or be plotted into bar chart format. The bar chart emphasizes that India and Europe grew at the same rate.

Picking the Right Tool for the Job

Now that you know which results you want to display, you'll need to choose the most appropriate tool for displaying your data. The most frequently used graphs for business communications are pie, bar, and line graphs.

Sometimes though, the best chart is no chart at all. If you only have one key message for your slide or the big message is just a number, why bother putting it in a chart? You could possibly increase the impact of your slide by eliminating the chart altogether. But which slide is more effective at comparing pet preferences?

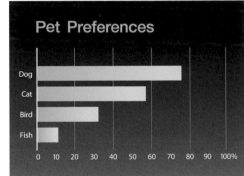

T!P
When several slides in a row have charts, line up the axes of the charts from slide to slide to avoid content that jumps around.

The left slide is effective at communicating the conclusion of the data. The slide on the right shows a comparison of the data.

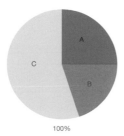

100%

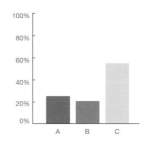

T!P
- Always start your first data set for a pie chart at the 12 o'clock position.

- Limit a pie chart to eight sections. More is too many to differentiate on a slide.

- Percentages on a pie chart must add up to 100%.

Pie charts work only for showing large differences in proportion, especially percentages. Use them when you want to show all of the parts that make up a whole, or compare the percentages of one set to the percentages of another.

Bar charts are visually more precise than pie charts, and can accommodate larger data sets. Plus, you can stack them to add an additional set of data. Use them when you need to show precise relationships.

Which graph below should you use if you wanted the audience to determine whether Mid-Cap U.S. Stock or Small-Cap U.S. Stock has the greatest share?

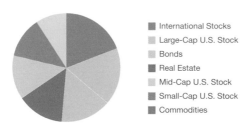

- International Stocks
- Large-Cap U.S. Stock
- Bonds
- Real Estate
- Mid-Cap U.S. Stock
- Small-Cap U.S. Stock
- Commodities

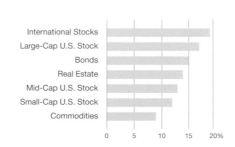

Investment Portfolio Breakdown

Investment Portfolio Breakdown

Images Courtesy of Stephen Few

Highlighting What's Important

Design rules for showing data on slides differ from the rules of displaying data on paper or through other media. Keep in mind that the purpose of slides is not to show all the data, but to communicate conclusions and insights. Slides can reference your handouts for the dense data. Think of a data chart in three layers.

Background

The background layer contains elements like tick marks, scales, legends, and grid lines. It provides context, scale, and reference for the data. Backgrounds should employ neutral colors.

Data

The data plotted on the slide is usually pulled from a data table. Data can be expressed through various chart types. Whatever the type, a chart should provide enough contrast to allow the audience to clearly distinguish information at a distance without straining.

Emphasis

The emphasis layer exists in the foreground and clearly highlights the key message from the data that is most important to your overall message for the slide. This concept might be a data point that's emphasized or a conclusion from the data.

Background | Data | Emphasis | Result

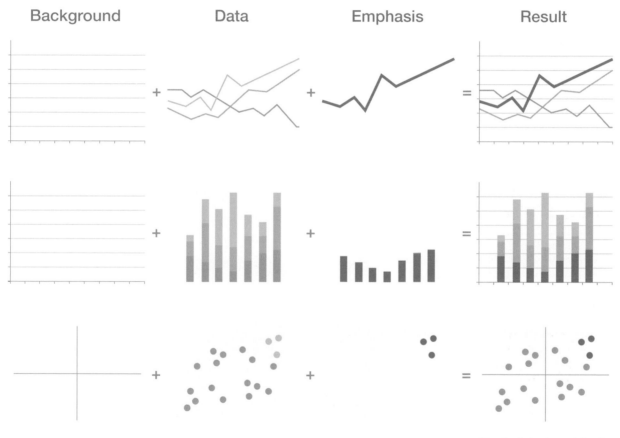

The final charts contain all the data but use contrast to draw the eye to the information that's most critical to the message.

Keeping It Simple

Save the decorations for the holidays. A common theme throughout this book has been the idea of simplicity, so it should come as no surprise that simplicity is important when displaying data for projection. In fact, simplicity is more important when displaying data, since the data itself can often confuse the viewer. It's equally critical to keep your data slides free of unnecessary clutter.

Unfortunately, presenters face other temptations when it comes to charts and graphs. No matter the software being used, there are a wealth of buttons, bullets, lines, ticks, gradients, borders, fills, and other chart decorations that can quickly overwhelm the data on the slide. Edward Tufte, author of *The Cognitive Style of Powerpoint*, refers to these as "chartjunk" or "PowerPoint Phluff". Do your best to avoid all unnecessary visual distractions and the message will come through much clearer.

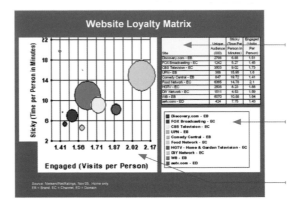

BEFORE

Data in this matrix is the same as the plotted data and can be removed.

Instead of a legend, put the identifier in the graph.

Modify the background elements so they are secondary to the data.

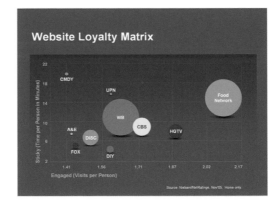

AFTER

Create more visual differentiation by increasing the space between sets of bars.

It's rarely necessary to show a table and accompanying chart on the same slide.

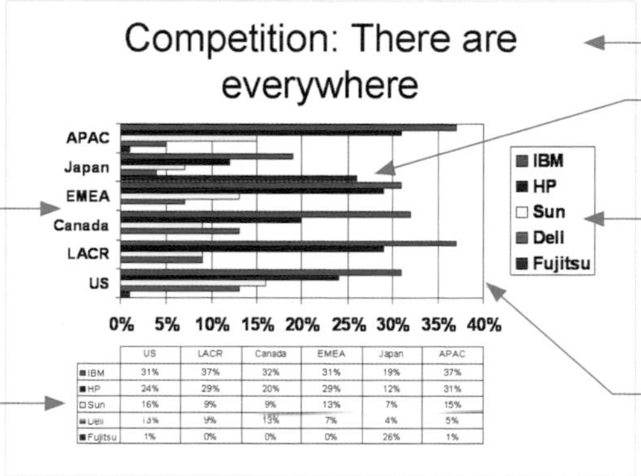

Competition: There are everywhere

Fix typo and title case

Reduce the number of colors and assign neutral colors to the secondary information.

Simplify the legend by removing the border, reducing the font size, and visually separating the primary information from the secondary information.

De-emphasize the background grid by lightening the color.

BEFORE

Competition Is Everywhere
Server Market Share by Region, 2003

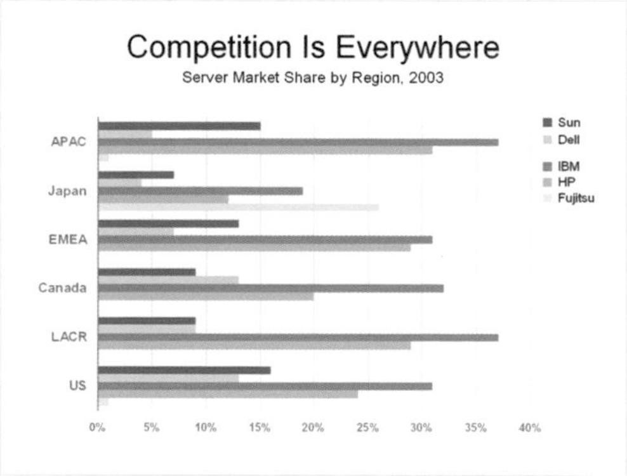

AFTER: The presenter wanted to emphasize how Sun and Dell were performing against each other.

Chart Makeovers

These chart makeovers have several elements that have changed. Removing the 3D effect makes the data appear more visually precise and changing the colors makes the data seem less harsh. You'll notice that in the before samples the dominant color was maroon. This color made sense because it was the key color of the company color palette. But shades of red are often used to annotate negative information in numbers especially in financial reporting.

Because it was important to incorporate the maroon in the palette, it was utilized in places like this world map to identify the location of support centers.

Pie Chart

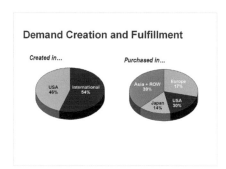

BEFORE 1

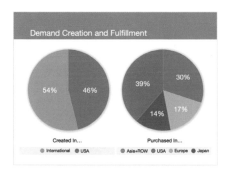

AFTER 1

Tilted pie charts tend to give more prominence to the data in the fore-ground. Also, the same color should represent the U.S. in both pie charts.

Vertical Bar Chart

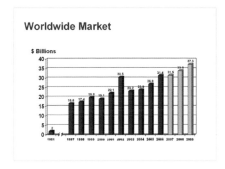

BEFORE 2

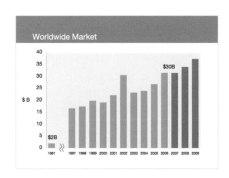

AFTER 2

Depth here serves no purpose. In fact, the depth can visually skew the data. A color distinction was used to emphasize the big take-away—the year they crossed the $30B mark.

Horizontal Bar Chart

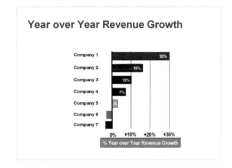

BEFORE 3

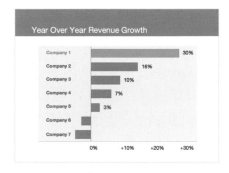

AFTER 3

Using too many bold colors obscures the focal point. Making the chart lon-ger horizontally helps emphasize the dominant growth of Company 1.

Case Study: Healthy Waters
Calling to Action with Images

Too often, information loses its impact—and presenters risk losing their audiences—because it isn't expressed as effectively as it could be. Put another way, emphasis is commonly placed on what the information is, rather than how it is best communicated.

It would have been tempting for Dr. Mike Magee to craft a presentation loaded with statistics and proof points that incorporate his years of research and analysis, but he understood that for change to happen, people need to be moved emotionally to act. Presenting his findings using a standard bullet points and bar graphs approach wouldn't accomplish that goal.

When your cause depends on empathy to move people to act, using the most compelling images is important. Using photos that are raw and real will motivate an audience to become involved. Dig through as many images as necessary to find the ones that elicit an emotional response.

www.healthy-waters.org

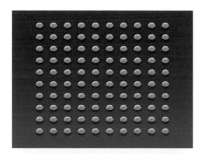

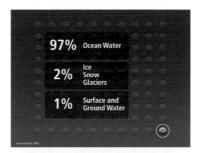

Most people default to the built-in charting features when faced with statistics. However, because of the critical nature of this message, the designers' intent was to imbue each slide with emotional appeal. Icons instead of numbers show the disparity in water usage around the world. The 100 drops of water represent 100% of the water on earth; animation of the water drops dissolving reveals that only 1% of our total water is fresh water.

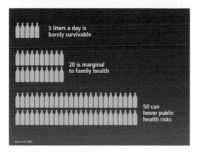

Bullet points aren't mandatory in a presentation; they're only one option for displaying text. These statistics have more impact because they're expressed separately and as large statements, rather than competing with other content on the slide.

To create maximum impact, designers considered the type of information being conveyed, and applied one of three techniques to it:

Illustrate Statistics: People's retention of data increases when they can "see the numbers." Various icons bring the information to life.

Isolate Text: Slides crowded with lengthy bullet points seldom communicate effectively. Pace the information by spreading it across multiple slides to increase its impact.

Employ Actual Photos: Stock imagery often fails because it lacks content. Real photos may not always be easy to look at, but they possess credibility and import that staged images do not.

Determining what information to present is only half the challenge; molding that information into an effective communication tool is the difference between good and great.

Photos should tell stories, show cause and effect, and engage audiences emotionally.

CHAPTER 5

Thinking Like a Designer

The Value of Design

The October 2007 *Fast Company*'s letter from the editor featured an intriguing chart depicting how design contributes to the bottom line. The Design Council compared a portfolio of 63 design-driven British companies and how they beat the broader market:

To quote the letter, "Studies have shown that design-oriented firms in all kinds of industries outperform their more-traditional peers—that design and innovation go hand-in-hand with financial success."

It's easy to tell when a company has design as a systemic value system. From product design to slides, you can tell which companies cherish design and value their brand.

What is a "design-oriented" firm? Companies like Apple, Target, Procter & Gamble, and Dyson all have design as a core part of their value-system.

This is not to say that dressing up your presentations will cause your stock to increase. Indeed, dressing up anything is counterintuitive to good design.

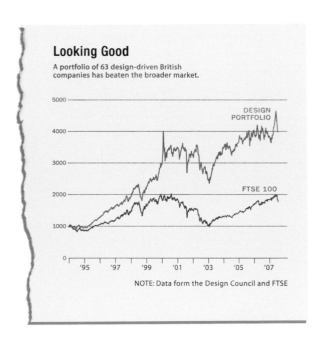

Looking Good

A portfolio of 63 design-driven British companies has beaten the broader market.

NOTE: Data form the Design Council and FTSE

You can also tell that these companies value their customers. Design is not solely about making things aesthetically pleasing, although that is part of it. Design, at its core, is about solving problems. And whatever that problem is—from squeezing oranges to running faster to communicating effectively—designers strive to help users solve their dilemma in the most convenient, simple, and elegant way. Essentially, designers focus on the experience, making it as beautiful and memorable as possible.

To succeed as a presenter, you must think like a designer.

Every decision a designer makes is intentional. Reason and logic underpin the placement of visual elements. Meaning underscores the order and hierarchy of ideas. Previous chapters highlighted the importance of understanding your audience, honing your key ideas and messages, and expressing yourself through appropriate diagrams and data. Now it's time to put those theories into practice. And though it is scant substitute for a formal design education, these next few chapters give nondesigners a design baseline that they can refer to when confronted by the empty expanse of a virgin slide.

Revealing Yourself Through Design Decisions

When my husband and I hired a life coach to facilitate the writing of our life mission statements, it became one of the greatest clarifying exercises I've ever done.

It also enriched our marriage. The coach guided us through several exercises, peeling back our psychological layers like an onion, to reveal our core values—the most critical element of a life mission statement. At its heart, it comes down to what you value, what you do, and for whom you do it.

One of the exercises involved scanning several pages of verbs to uncover how we perceived our individual motivations: after all, the most important component of the life statement is the verb. Out of the entire list, we were asked to narrow our selections to three. Unfortunately, after perusing the list I began to panic because I couldn't find my verbs anywhere. I always felt I was different but even with hundreds of verbs I didn't want to settle. I got a bit choked up and apologized for being odd. The coach asked me what my verbs were and without blinking I said, "conquer and liberate." He thought those choices were great. Was he kidding?

My husband, on the other hand, found his verb in the second column and didn't need to continue. When he revealed his verb, our worlds suddenly made sense. We're as opposite as two individuals could be. His life verb was "relax." Finally, it made sense why we both wanted to approach vacations, finances, child-rearing, and business differently.

If we were to express our life mission statements visually, they would be very different. One might consider this a type of personal brand. Mine would have colors that are fiery and passionate while his would be serene. My typeface would be big block letters so the troops can read the flag in battle, whereas his would be a script font overlaying a putting green. You get the point. The design decisions you make represent you and feed your audience's perceptions of who you are.

Most branding exercises employ adjectives to describe an organization. But they only tell you what it is. We prefer to define what it does. Circle a few verbs that resonate with you.

What do these verbs tell you about the character of your company?

Accomplish	Confirm	Enlist	Launch	Present	Serve
Acquire	Connect	Enliven	Lead	Produce	Share
Adopt	Consider	Entertain	Liberate	Progress	Speak
Advance	Contact	Enthuse	Light	Promise	Stand
Affirm	Construct	Excite	Live	Promote	Summon
Alleviate	Continue	Explore	Love	Provide	Support
Amplify	Counsel	Express	Make	Pursue	Surrender
Appreciate	Create	Extend	Manifest	Realize	Sustain
Ascend	Decide	Facilitate	Master	Receive	Take
Associate	Defend	Finance	Mature	Reclaim	Tap
Believe	Delight	Forgive	Measure	Reduce	Teach
Bestow	Deliver	Foster	Mediate	Refine	Team
Brighten	Devise	Franchise	Mentor	Reform	Touch
Build	Direct	Further	Model	Regard	Trade
Call	Discover	Gather	Mold	Relax	Translate
Cause	Discuss	Generate	Motivate	Relate	Travel
Claim	Distill	Give	Move	Release	Understand
Choose	Distribute	Grant	Negotiate	Rely	Use
Coach	Draft	Heal	Nurture	Remember	Utilize
Collect	Dream	Hold	Open	Renew	Value
Combine	Drive	Identify	Participate	Resonate	Venture
Command	Educate	Illuminate	Pass	Respect	Verbalize
Communicate	Elect	Implement	Perform	Restore	Work
Compel	Embrace	Improvise	Persuade	Revise	Worship
Compete	Enjoy	Integrate	Play	Sacrifice	Write
Compliment	Encourage	Involve	Possess	Safeguard	Yield
Compose	Endow	Keep	Practice	Satisfy	
Conceive	Engage	Know	Praise	Save	
Conquer	Enhance	Labor	Prepare	Sell	

Case Study: Al Gore
A Brand Makeover

In addition to his other prominent achievements—serving as Vice President, winning an Academy Award, garnering the Nobel Peace Prize—Al Gore has done more than any other individual to legitimize multimedia presentations as one of the most compelling communication vehicles on the planet. He has focused the world's attention on climate change, and it all began with a slide show. He has proven that presentations can tap emotions to incite grass roots change. He is the poster child for the transformative powers of a great presentation. Ultimately, his approach was truly fit for the silver screen.

Gore's journey started when he dusted off his 35mm slide carousel from the '70s and transformed it into a multimedia presentation. By early 2003 he was traveling the world delivering his revived passion for the environment. Long before the idea of a movie was on the table, he delivered his presentation at hundreds of venues. Climate change was yet to be a ubiquitous cause. Watching Gore on stage was transformational. This wasn't the stodgy former Vice President that people had come to expect from the campaign trail. From the moment Mr. Gore took the stage, he was fired up, passionately saving the world from its own burning fate. He paced, yelled (a bit), and was ultimately quite charming. This man had a mission. He was alive, charismatic, fluid, candid, and animated. Without exception, his audience left feeling informed and inspired. You could sense the momentum building.

Mr. Gore elevated his visual strategy and staging choreography to a whole new level. Now that the film *An Inconvenient Truth* has reached a mass audience, many people across the country and around the world have changed their perceptions of him as well. He has achieved a significant brand makeover. The July 2007 issue of *Fast Company* reported:

"In one of the most remarkable personal turnarounds of all time, Mr. Gore reinvented the way people respond to him. He's gone from guarded Washington politician to a Hollywood celebrity to a celebrated international leader."

Ellen McGirt
Fast Company

Beyond possessing a visceral, long-nurtured passion for the cause, much of his success can be attributed to the significant investment he makes in internalizing the subject matter and rehearsing the delivery. He also seeks and takes expert guidance.

No one can ignore his personal communication transformation. He passionately knows his content, his slides add value to his story, and he is comfortable in his delivery. He's impacting our world, one slide at a time.

Al Gore
Former Vice President of the United States

U.S. Renewable Energy Future

Biomass ■ Solar ■ Wind ■ Hydro ■ Geothermal

Energy Production (Quads)

Designing Effective Slides

Approaching the design of a slide can seem daunting. Effective slide design hinges on mastery of three things: arrangement, visual elements, and movement. These will be covered in the following chapters:

Arrangement	Visual Elements	Movement
contrast hierarchy unity space proximity flow	background color text images	timing pace distance direction eye flow

Presentations broadcast information to an audience in much the same way as a radio transmission. Thus, think of a presentation's slides as a signal. Can you remember when your favorite junior high song came on the radio but there was so much static interference that you turned off the radio rather than hear your fond memories garbled? Strength and clarity determine how well information is conveyed.

Like a poor radio signal, slides are susceptible to interference and noise, clouding the intended message and compromising the audience's ability to discern meaning and intent.

The arrangement, visual elements, and movement of a slide function either as a signal, delivering information clearly and directly, or as noise, interfering with the message and causing the viewer to tune out.

In the vast majority of cases, a slide fails not due to stylistic issues, but due to its fundamental construction. Thus, the most important tool in a presenter's arsenal is a strong familiarity with the mechanics of a well-designed slide.

"People have a hard time coping with excessive cognitive strain. There is simply a limit to a person's ability to process new information efficiently and effectively. Understanding can be hard enough without the excessive and nonessential bombardment by our visuals that are supposed to be playing a supportive role."

Garr Reynolds
Author, *Presentation Zen*

CHAPTER 6

Arranging Elements

Placement of Elements Creates Meaning

Quite possibly, how slides are arranged has the most impact on whether a slide's message is visually clear. Arrangement tells a story. Based on the arrangement decisions a designer makes, a slide can prompt feelings of tension, confusion, and agitation; conversely, it can maximize clarity by employing the following:

Contrast
The audience can identify the main point quickly.

Flow
The audience knows the order in which to process the information.

Hierarchy
The audience sees the relationship between elements.

Unity
The audience senses that the information belongs together.

Proximity
The audience perceives meaning from the location of elements.

Whitespace
The audience has visual breathing room.

These are the tools of the slide design trade. It's tough to assemble a great slide without paying close attention to each of these issues. Luckily, these are intuitive concepts. That may already by familiar to you.

Slides begin and end with ideas. It's your job to take these invisible, abstract ideas and determine how they can be best represented in a tangible, visual form. It's the presenter's responsibility to ensure that the audience is guided through this invisible world by making ideas easy to decode.

Many presenters don't understand arrangement as a principle. They will put everything on one slide and assign them equal value. It is critical to determine which visual elements should have prominence so they attract attention first.

Create dominance with some elements and practice restraint with others. Force yourself to make a decision about the priority of the information.

It's laziness on the presenter's part to put everything on one slide.

Overcrowding the slide doesn't add to the clarity of the message.

Contrast: Identifying the Main Point Quickly

Audiences need contrast. Viewers immediately perceive the difference between the attributes of two or more things, and this focuses their attention. There are many ways to create contrast on a slide; here are some examples:

size   shape   shade   color   proximity

Establishing a relationship between slide elements is an important first step. The contrast in the size of the following text, for example, draws the eye to the larger text as if it's a title or context for the text block. Regardless of where the text is placed, the larger text is perceived as the most important.

Lorem Ipsum

Putpat, consed tio od
tat lum nit autpatem
diamcommy.

Putpat, consed tio od
tat lum nit autpatem
diamcommy.

Lorem Ipsum

San velenibh ex. Et
vent wisl ulla feugue

Lorem Ipsum

tionsequis nostrud.

Creating contrast in a body of text can be done with size, but also through the use of color. Some versions of the Bible highlight the words of Jesus in red. Below, a quote from Edward Tufte, author of *Visual Explanations*, has a key phrase highlighted in red.

Tufte's design strategy of the smallest effective difference uses contrast wisely yet subtly and only when necessary. He says: ...the idea is to use just notable differences, visual elements that make a clear difference but no more—contrasts that are definitive, effective and minimal.

A common mistake presenters make is assigning contrast unintentionally. Virtually any stylistic difference between two elements suggests something to the viewer on either a conscious or subconscious level. Unintentional contrast can confuse the intended message at best, and contradict it at worst. Remember, all stylistic choices have the potential to suggests importance, urgency, and value. As a result, you should base all such choices on a well-defined purpose.

"Without contrast you're dead."

Paul Rand
Designer

Flow: Ordering How the Information Is Processed

A typical Western reading pattern runs from left to right and top to bottom. Readers are conditioned to start at the top left and scan back and forth across content in a Z-shaped path until they've processed the information.

Jerry Weissman, author of *Presenting to Win*, calls this the conditioned carriage return, as it mimics the movement of the carriage on an old fashioned typewriter.

Readers move their eyes back and forth across a slide until they feel they have identified everything on the slide. They then will assign meaning to the information. If, to make your point, your graphic needs to flow in a direction that's counter-intuitive to natural eye movement, build it over time, with discrete elements appearing in the order you want your audience to process it. Alternately, use a symbol or arrow that clearly marks a starting point. The audience should be able to understand the intended order in which to process the information, without ever feeling lost or overwhelmed.

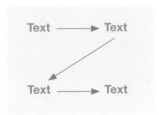

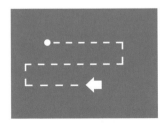

Using an arrow to mark the starting point draws attention to it where to begin.

Size and perspective indicate the bottom left as the starting point here.

You should organize slides to guide the audience's eyes through the content in an obvious way. This principle applies not only to text, but to diagrams and images as well.

When using images of people, make sure that they're looking at the content instead of looking away, or fleeing it.

 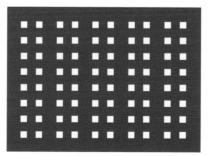

At a glance, the audience should be able to determine whether to read data charts horizontally or vertically.

T!P

- Avoid more than three layers of information on a single plane.

- Create points of interest (one main point and up to two sub-points).

- Develop flow within the slide intentionally.

- Choose images and diagrams with clear directional flow.

- Select images that flow toward the focal point on the slide or toward the next slide.

Hierarchy: Seeing Relationships Between Elements

An audience processes hierarchy almost as quickly as contrast. Visual hierarchy, simply put, defines the structure formed when relationships are applied to a set of elements. A simple example of this is the relationship of a title to its body text. Within the hierarchy, the title is the parent and the text is the child. Just like a family lineage, each element in a hierarchy is the child of the element above it, or the parent of the element below it.

Most significant

Lorem Ipsum

Least significant

- Lorem Ipsum
  Ting ex et utatue digna lutpat lutatem

- Lorem Ipsum
  Ting ex et utatue digna lutpat lutatem

- Lorem Ipsum
  Ting ex et utatue digna lutpat lutatem

Lorem Ipsum

- **Lorem Ipsum**
  Ting ex et utatue digna lutpat lutatem

- **Lorem Ipsum**
  Ting ex et utatue digna lutpat lutatem

- **Lorem Ipsum**
  Ting ex et utatue digna lutpat lutatem

Size and location are used together to indicate a decreasing significance from the top left to the bottom right.

Making the bullet points heavier than the title disrupts the logical flow. The audience would have a hard time making sense of it.

Not coincidentally then, the visual structure precisely mirrors the structure of the information it represents. For example, the following diagrams radiate from a core. The core is what binds the elements together and establishes the parent-child relationship. Modifying the size and proximity of the objects changes the meaning behind the relationships and tells a story about their relative importance.

Changing the Size and Proximity of Objects Modifies Their Visual Story

Elements Are Equal
Story: We all need to rally together as a team around this goal for which you're all equally suited.

Parent Dominates
Story: We all need to rally together as a team around this goal which is more important than activities at the team or individual level.

Child Dominates
Story: We all need to rally together as a team around this goal and some of the teams will have bigger challenges than others.

When your presentation is over, you want the audience to walk away understanding their mission. If you don't intentionally provide that message, the audience will create meaning based on their own interpretation of the information. Make sure that you've presented the graphical hierarchy of your message accurately.

Unity: Sensing the Structure of Information

You can achieve unity through structure (grid), look (graphical style), and theme (big idea). Here, you'll focus on the grid.

Since every brand and presenter is unique, the grid used should reflect you or your company.

A grid system provides a flexible way to organize content.

To guide the organization of content, create rectanglar regions for placement of elements. Each region is a container for an element, such as a block of text or an image.

Placing objects within a grid anchors the individual elements so they don't bounce around or appear like they were positioned haphazardy or randomly. This stability helps the audience identify patterns in the placement of content. Having text and graphics show up in the same place, anchored to the same points, helps an audience anticipate where content will appear. Additionally, grids ensure that across multiple slides of a similar layout, elements don't appear to "jump." For instance, if three consecutive slides feature graphs, the location of their axes should remain constant even though the data changes.

Grids also help streamline design decisions for corporations where thousands of employees develop slides independently. Organizations benefit from the ability to re-use slides when they look similar and follow a basic grid system.

Once you've sketched out a grid that you like, pencil in where you might place images, text, and objects. Be sure to leave plenty of the tiles open to preserve clear space. Now, draw the grid lines in your presentation application and place it on the master slide, being sure to remove the grid when you've completed the design process. To speed development of your presentation in the future, save the grid as a tool by pasting it into a new file or saving it on a slide at the very back of your deck.

The slides below were created in four different grid patterns. The orange grids with gray boxes serve as keys for the slides beneath them. You can see how the elements fit into the grid.

Three Column

Planning Process
Establish Initiatives

Three Outcomes
Building Momentum

SHARED OBJECTIVES 1   SHARED VALUES 2   SHARED RESULTS 3

Four Column

HR Challenges in Q1

Define quarterly objectives · Align culture to initiatives · Deploy training programs

Project Forecast
- Team continues to practice our process until flawless
- Launch occurs in Q1 and then will work against the wind

Smooth sailing for the next two months!

Five Column

Tracking Urban Migration

49%   29%   13%   1900 1950 2005

Urbanization

Fibonacci

Your Zen Retreat
Use decorative accents to add eastern inspired flavors

East Meets West
Modern Home Design

■ Graphic
■ Text

These slides look uniform because the grid gives them structure.

The Creative Professional

Case Study: Adobe
Controlling Elements with a Grid

Call it the price of success for Adobe Systems. Being the number one developer of software applications for graphic designers means that every piece of collateral, every package design, every advertisement will be scrutinized by the experts, who are also the customers.

The same goes for presentations, only this time it is personal: imagine not connecting with an audience because they're distracted by the slide layouts. At best, the audience will be mildly critical; at worst, the presenter stands to lose some credibility. The solution? Combine the best in presentation design with the fundamentals of graphic design. The results showcase Adobe's commitment to the industry they transformed.

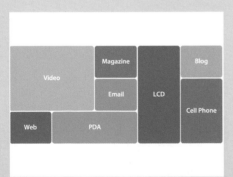

Derived from their product packaging, the fresh color palette reflects Adobe's brand. The dynamic grid provides a way to introduce photography through a series of builds.

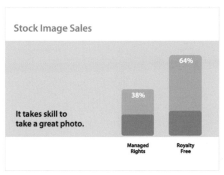

Stock Image Sales

It takes skill to
take a great photo.

64%

38%

Managed
Rights

Royalty
Free

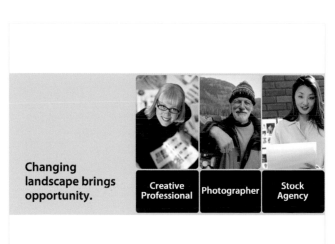

Changing
landscape brings
opportunity.

Creative
Professional

Photographer

Stock
Agency

Cross Media Publishing

Breaking the grid can
be an effective way to
focus attention on
specific elements. But
make sure that this is
the exception and not
the rule: overuse will
diminish its impact.

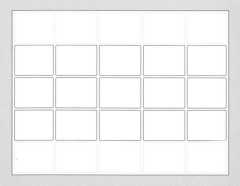

Adobe's presentations rely on an underlying 5x5 grid to
determine the placement of text, imagery, and objects.
Though the shapes and sizes of elements vary, the regu-
larity of layouts produces a sense of structure and solid-
ity. Additionally, leaving the top and bottom channels
empty creates a more cinematic feeling while providing
space for titles and similar information.

Proximity: Perceiving Meaning from Location

When more than a single element or person appears in a scene, their placement relative to each other tells a secondary story to the image itself. Haphazardly placed elements can leave an impression different than the one intended.

Space Proximity

You should place elements associated with each other intentionally. Leave nothing to chance. How the objects are assembled communicates antagonism or protagonism, chaos or order, decline or growth, and so on. Ultimately, your goal is to preempt the audience from making unintended interpretations.

unite • fragment

order • chaos

equal • unequal

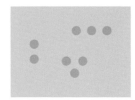

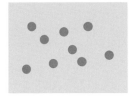

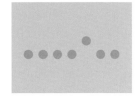

Other Relationships

symmetric • asymmetric
balanced • imbalanced
consistent • inconsistent
clear • obscure
spacious • crowded
sequential • random
understated • exaggerated
attractive • repellent
deep • wide
static • active
distributed • consolidated
near • far

People Proximity

In the theatre, directors position actors on stage in support of the story. For instance, consider the different placement of people in the following frames. Each placement takes on meaning, even without context or knowledge of the narrative of which they might be a part. The following concepts were inspired by Robert Horn's seminal work, *Visual Language*.

The subject at the left or right edge is often perceived as weak, relative to the subject closer to the center.

Subjects on opposite sides of the screen are distantly related or perhaps antagonists.

Subjects in the center are perceived as closely related.

A subject at the bottom is frequently perceived as submissive, weak, vulnerable. A subject at the top is often seen as dominant, powerful.

Isolated subjects convey more visual weight than grouped subjects.

A subject with a lot of space in the frame suggests freedom.

Clustered subjects that are out of balance in the scene emphasize action.

Whitespace: Getting Visual Breathing Room

The visible elements of a slide often receive the most focus. But you need to pay equal attention to how much space you leave open. This is often referred to as whitespace, negative space, or clear space.

Whitespace isn't necessarily white; it refers to the areas of the slide left unused. It could be the empty areas that separate elements from one another or the drama created when an element is set in vast amounts of space. The book so far has discussed the role of hierarchy, flow, and proximity, but until now, the role of whitespace has been merely implied.

Inexperienced presenters often think whitespace is expendable—especially when they need to incorporate unwieldy amounts of content that's "too important" to be distilled or simplified despite its cumbersome density. After all, whitespace by definition carries no information, so what's the harm in filling it up? The harm is that audiences find these slides difficult to comprehend. Whitespace is as much an element of a slide as titles, bullets, and diagrams. In large part, the use or misuse of whitespace determines a slide's effectiveness.

Generally, any slide that needs to sacrifice whitespace to make room for content is packed too tightly. When a slide is expected to present more information than it can comfortably hold, it is no longer the right tool for the job.

Ask yourself, "What can I take away that won't change the meaning?" or "Where can I split the content into more than one slide?" Keep in mind that a slide's value is determined not by the amount of information it contains, but by how clearly it communicates its message.

It's okay to have clear space—clutter is a failure of design.

Breaking the content into three slides is much more effective for audiences than being thrown into a one slide mess, and expecting them to interpret the data all at once. Spreading the information across three slides doesn't solve the density problem alone. Displaying the elements sequentially guides the audience through the information.

BEFORE: The slide contains dense information that requires effort to process. The lack of whitespace between various elements makes it hard to derive meaning from content. We divided the content on this slide into three slides shown bellow.

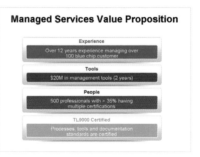

AFTER: By distributing the elements across multiple slides, each receives the attention it deserves—and the audience benefits from a better understanding of the concepts.

Case Study: Garr Reynolds
A Lesson on Space

By far one of the most significant influencers of great presentation design, Garr Reynolds is transforming presenters through his blog and book, both titled *Presentation Zen*. Reynolds' insights and clever wit systematically cover sound principles for content, design, and delivery.

He believes that "design isn't about decoration or about ornamentation. Design is about making communication as easy and clear for the viewer as possible." Reynolds has his own signature style of large, striking images and enormous amounts of empty space that lead the eye.

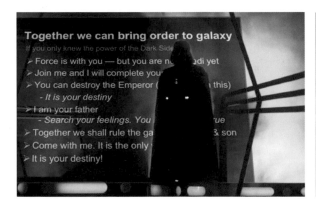

Here Garr's blog spoofs the presentation styles of Darth Vader and Yoda.

Even though this is a quote from Reynolds' book, you can probably picture Yoda saying: "Empty space is not nothing; it is a powerful something. Learn to see it."

"A Zen garden is also a lesson in simplicity. Open space without ornamentation, a few rocks carefully selected and placed, raked gravel. Beautiful. Simple. The Zen garden is very different from gardens in the West that are absolutely filled with beauty, so much beauty, in fact, that we miss much of it. Presentations are a bit like this. Sometimes, we're presented with so much visual and auditory stimulation in such a short time that we end up understanding very little and remembering even less."

Garr Reynolds
Author, *Presentation Zen*

garden photo © Markuz Wernli Saito

Finding Beauty in the Design Around You

Designers create meaning by carefully arranging elements. It's never a haphazard splatter of text and graphics; there is intent and that intent creates meaning. Whether that meaning informs or creates a feeling or structure, it all serves a purpose.

Take a moment and study your environment. Look at graphic design, architecture, and product design. Ask yourself why the designers made the decisions they did. Why did they use the typeface, colors, or particular placement of the elements? Then determine the contrast, flow, hierarchy, unity, proximity, and space.

These elements exist even in nature. Look for them.

Processing the beauty around you is important. When you watch a film, look through a magazine, hike across a spring meadow, attend a ballet, or visit a museum, study the beauty and grow in appreciation for things that are beautiful.

If you visually ingest beautiful design, you will be able to output beauty. But it takes study and contemplation of what makes those things beautiful.

Each art form has considerations for how to arrange elements to create meaning and beauty.

Japanese flower arrangement is designed to create harmony and balance in how the visual elements (flora in this case) are assembled.

At the onset, the designer plans out exactly the journey they want the eyes to travel across the arrangement. The designer controls the eye movement by stripping all but the essential blossoms out of the arrangement. Similarly, you should remove everything on a slide that doesn't bring emphasis to your point.

CHAPTER 7

Using Visual Elements: Background, Color, and Text

The Ingredients of a Great Slide

Now that you know how to arrange elements on a slide, it's time to identify the elements you'll work with. This section covers best practices to use when determining the elements. There really aren't many decisions to make about them: that's why selecting them thoughtfully and carefully is important. The four visual elements are background, color, text, and images. The first three are covered in this section, and images are covered in the next chapter.

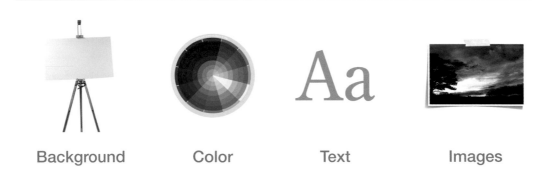

| Background | Color | Text | Images |

Each ingredient—background, color, text, and images—determines how your slide elements will look and requires that you make key design decisions. Once you've decided how the elements will look, you can apply the principles from Chapter 6, "Arranging Elements."

There's one specific theme you need to keep at the forefront of your mind—consistency. Choose element styles and then stick with them. These elements actually become visual triggers of your brand. Whether your brand is just you or a major corporation, pick elements that you feel will resonate with your audience, and then stay consistent.

Still, every blue moon, there is also power in breaking the consistency. Let's say your slide design remains consistent for 20 slides. Then, to create a memorable visual moment, you incorporate something inconsistent with the rest of the slides. That inconsistency will stand out. However, if you break the rules all the time, you've lost your opportunity for visual emphasis.

Background

A background is a container or surface on which to place visual elements. It can incorporate anything you want, or it can have nothing on it at all.

You determine whether the surface is opaque or textured, and whether it has a light source, and from where it originates. But first you need to pry yourself away from the default templates with their preordained slide junk. Think through what is really required. What reflects your intent and personality? What reflects your company's brand? What will act in service to your information rather than compete with it? Consider approaching the background in a way never seen before.

Where does it say that every slide needs a logo? The people who have come to hear you speak most likely know who you work for. Use your first and last slides (called bumper slides) to identify yourself or company.

On the other hand, if your boss insists you put the logo on every slide, the lower right is the best place for it because you can wrap the right rag of text around it. After all, the same boss who wants the logo on every slide probably has so much text to shoehorn in, you need to wrap it.

Two of my pet peeves are folks who include their logo on every slide, and that animated paper clip in the Microsoft Office product suite.

Backgrounds Are a Surface for Digital Assets

Backgrounds are intended as a surface on which to place elements. They are not in themselves a work of art.

They are a setting, surface, or platform. In print design, designers start with a white or blank piece of paper and then place objects on it. You rarely see a brochure where every page has been covered with a crazy design like the one here.

A background creates a sense of space. That space should be open, spacious, and simple. A slide background is like real estate: it's very valuable, so build on it wisely. Avoid the trend to make the background ornamented, crowded, and distracting. Keep the background as simple and intentionally clean as possible. Your background is there to host your objects, not be an object.

Backgrounds should never compete with content.

The space inside the box is all that's usable.

This is an ineffectual slide template with useless ornamentation around the edges. The orange box highlights the active or "live" area of the slide that can be used for graphics. The designer of this template used at least one-third of the available real estate for meaningless graphical elements.

So now that you've seen a case for open space, what do you do with this nice large open canvas?

Ignore all the default masters and look through your company's marketing material to identify visual elements of the brand that are timeless. You can usually identify a grid system, line structures, bounding boxes, color palette, or visual elements that anchor the designs. Pick the more timeless elements that will never change. You can start there as a basis for the background design. If you don't work for a company, then the sky is the limit. However, your decisions still need to reflect your personality.

Traversing Flatland and Dimensions

You can create graphics in either a 2D or 3D space. But only pick one.

Using the presentation application as a 2D space would require that you place objects with little or no depth to them onto a flat background surface. It's very striking to have bold flat color and keep the visual elements flat as well. Minimizing depth minimizes complexity. Bold floods of color create a clean surface on which elements can be placed. The layout of this book uses a flat white surface that elements were placed on.

Once you begin to add elements with shadows, lighting, and depth, you're pretty committed to a 3D space. These effects can be as subtle as having images cast soft shadows, or as dramatic as the images on the opposite page.

Moving out of flatland takes courage and a commitment to keeping elements within the "laws of consistency" established by the background and setting. The moment you introduce a glisten or shadow, you've committed yourself to mimicking an environment that now has three dimensions. Highlight, shadows, depth, layers—everything in an environment is consistently influenced by the setting. To help reduce visual vertigo, use the laws of environmental consistency.

Laws of Environmental Consistency

1 Consistent vanishing point

2 Consistent light source

3 Consistent effect on the elements

Now that applications let users manipulate the light source and perspective, keeping it all consistent is more important than ever. Pick one light source and one vanishing point and stick with it throughout your entire file. To the right are examples of how to keep elements consistent.

www

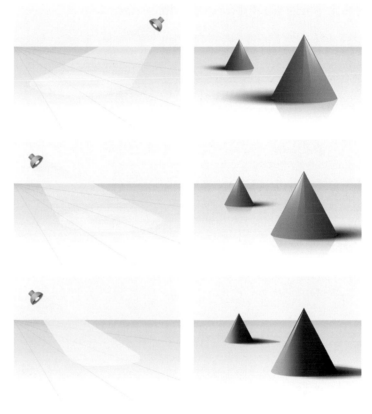

Notice how the cones become smaller to establish perspective. The shadows' angles are also consistent with the light source.

Here the cone has highlights on the left side as opposed to the lighting effect above.

In this setting the light is harsher so the highlights should be brighter and the shadows' edges more defined.

Creating a Sense of Space

Look at each slide as if it's an environment.

Many folks randomly place a hodge-podge of visual elements on their slides. This could make your audience feel lost in the space that you've created.

If each slide is an environment, then determining the influence that the environment has on your visual elements is critical. The elements need to map into the vanishing point and lighting you establish. Elements that don't fit can make the audience feel unsettled, because they're looking at an unnatural scene, and are thus subliminally frustrated. Think about what your objects would look like in real life with the depth and lighting you've established.

Scenes in real life occur in three dimensions, whereas on-screen they happen only in two. It's easy to make a 2D surface have depth by making some early, simple decisions. But maybe you think you didn't establish an environment. You did, whether intentional or not, the moment you drew a graphic. The style of that graphic determined its environment.

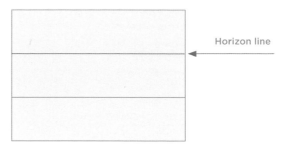

If you choose to go with a grid of thirds, consider using one of the lines as a horizon line.

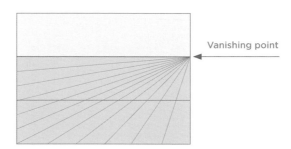

Draw lines that converge at a point on the horizon. This simulates the vanishing point.

Now that you've determined a horizon and vanishing point, those decisions will influence the objects you place into this environment. The features of the objects you place in the scene need to match what's already there. To the right you can see that the angles on the sides of the cubes change based on the horizon line and vanishing point. Create objects that follow the same vanishing point and horizon line. Do not mix and match the angles of objects in the same scene. If you do, the scene won't look natural.

This last environmental example has no horizon or vanishing point. It's an isometric grid.

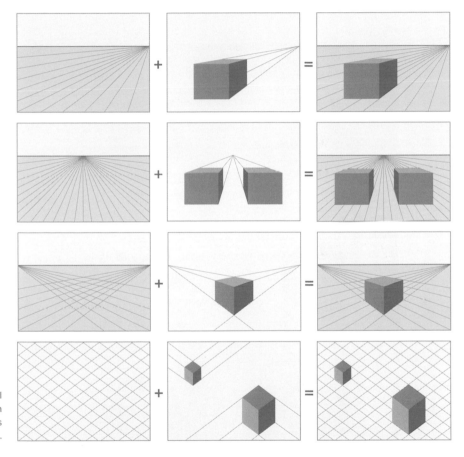

Determining the Light Source

Next, determine the source of your lighting. The source will dictate how light is cast on your background. Determining how light affects your background also influences how light is cast on the objects placed on the background. Light creates shadows and highlights.

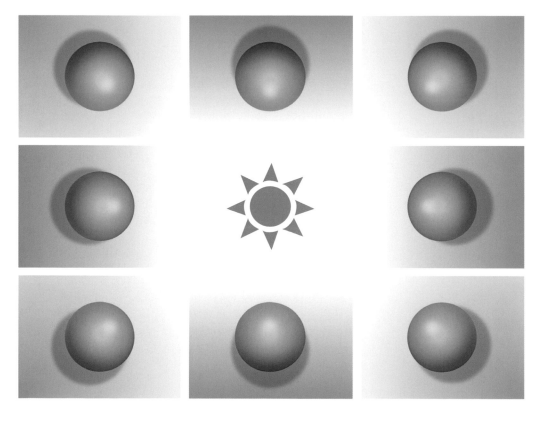

These eight backgrounds have a light source that shines across them. When you place elements into these backgrounds, their highlights and shadows follow the same source of light. For your background, select one angle for the light source and stick with it throughout the presentation.

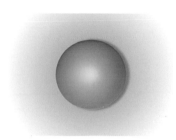

Adding a soft, circular shadow behind the sphere makes it look as if it is hovering over a surface or in front of a wall, and that you're looking straight at it.

An elliptical shadow placed at the bottom of the sphere makes it look as if it's sitting on a surface.

Adding a reflection below the sphere makes it look as if it's sitting on a very shiny surface.

T!P

- The background is a surface, stage, or backdrop—not the main focus.

- What's in the background should be subordinate to the real content.

- Avoid adding photos or images to the background. It distracts the audience; they will try to process what the image is and why it has been obscured.

Color

Color is crucial to your presentation. It sets a tone and helps establish what the audience will expect. It helps communicate what type of journey you will be taking them on. Is it an exciting journey or a serious or dangerous one? Pick colors that properly represent you, your company, and your stance.

Who is your audience?
Determine colors that appeal to the target audience and avoid colors that won't resonate with them.

What industry are you in?
Review the colors of your competitors to ensure that your chosen palette helps you stand out in your field. Also avoid colors that are negative in your industry. For example red should be avoided for a financial institution, but would be okay for a blood bank.

Who are you?
Pick colors that reflect your personality. Whether your brand is vivid and exciting, or repetitive and conservative, select colors that represent it.

Our family went on a train ride from San Jose to Chicago. Amtrak times it perfectly so that the train arrives in Denver right at sunset. This leg was to be the highlight of the journey—descending the Rocky Mountains into the Colorado basin. But unbeknownst to us, during the night the pass over the Rockies was blocked, and in Salt Lake City we were rerouted through southern Wyoming.

The hope of an entire day meandering through the Rockies and descending into Denver was shattered. Instead of a vivid, vibrant, and exciting palette, we had a consistent, monotonous, and conservative palette. Not that a conservative palette is bad, it just didn't match our expectations. Try to meet your audience's expectations.

The Colorado skies were supposed to be the highlight of our journey.

Unfortunately miles of bland landscape deflated the mood of the trip.

About the Color Wheel

Understanding and using the color wheel helps you choose a harmonious palette.

The color wheel helps you visualize the relationships that colors have to one another. Microsoft's PowerPoint and Apple's Keynote applications base their color wheels on the one that Sir Isaac Newton discovered. The wheel uses three primary colors, red, yellow and blue, spaced evenly apart. Blending those colors creates the full color wheel, as shown on the right-hand page.

Each pie slice of the wheel has tints and shades of a single hue (true color). The hue on this wheel is four rings out from the center. The colors toward the center of the wheel have white added to the hue, called *tints,* whereas the rings of colors on the outside of the hue have black added to them to create a *shade* of the color.

Presentation applications reference the color wheel's logic in their color picker tools, which is a good reason to understand the color wheel itself.

You can select colors for your palette anywhere in the wheel with any saturation of color, but make sure that it contrasts and projects well. There is a bit of a science to creating a pleasing palette.

Apple's Keynote Color Picker

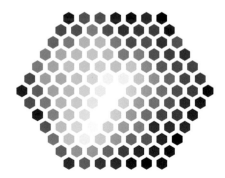

Microsoft's PowerPoint Color Picker

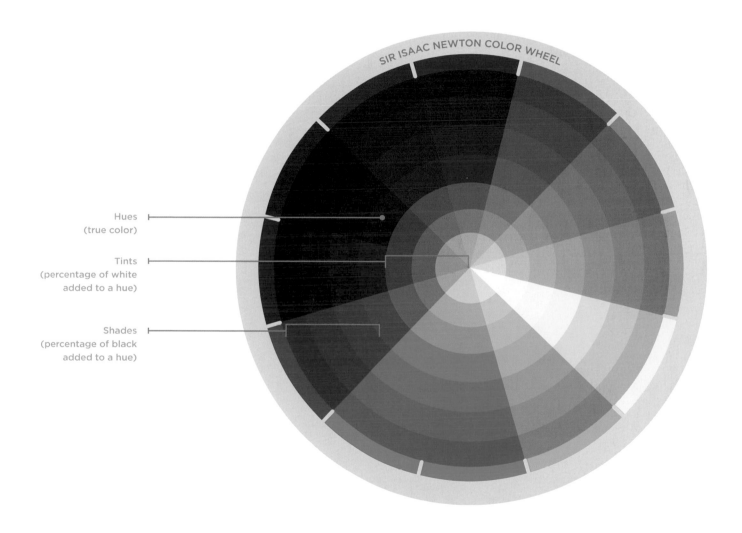

SIR ISAAC NEWTON COLOR WHEEL

Hues
(true color)

Tints
(percentage of white
added to a hue)

Shades
(percentage of black
added to a hue)

Using the Power of Color

Monochromatic

Using variations of the same color can create a striking palette, but it's difficult to use color effectively without adding black, white, and shades of gray for contrast. Select colors with a broad range of tints and shades to provide enough contrast.

Analogous

Selecting colors that are touching in the wheel creates a narrow, harmonious color scheme. Similar to monochromatic colors, analogous colors provide a predominantly warm or cool feeling, depending on where they lie on the wheel.

Complementary

Colors from the opposite ends of the wheel provide the most contrast. If you can stave off the temptation to add more colors, limit them to only two to create a powerful (or even startling) look. But arrange them wisely so they don't clash.

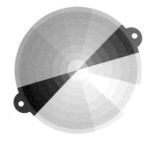

Earthy

R 72	R 101	R 144
G 107	G 141	G 193
B 28	B 43	B 62

Strong

R 144	R 215	R 243
G 25	G 32	G 113
B 28	B 39	B 84

Powerful

R 136	R 196	R 198
G 20	G 22	G 68
B 119	B 28	B 31

Calm

R 0	R 0	R 136
G 172	G 175	G 198
B 179	B 113	B 91

Athletic

R 202	R 0
G 108	G 84
B 24	B 150

Feminine

R 191	R 188
G 86	G 211
B 139	B 87

Split Complementary

This variation of the complementary scheme uses two colors on either side of a directly complementary color. These colors have high visual contrast but with less visual tension than purely complementary colors.

Triadic

Three colors equally spaced around the color wheel create vivid visual interest. Some of the palettes are bold while others are more refined. You can modify this method by using a light tint or dark shade of one of the three colors instead of the pure hue.

Tetradic

This scheme is popular because it offers strong visual contrast while retaining harmony. It uses two pairs of complementary colors. It's difficult to harmonize this scheme if all four hues are used in equal amounts. Pick a dominant color for your design and use the others to support the main one.

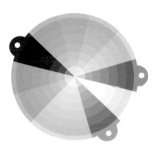

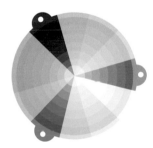

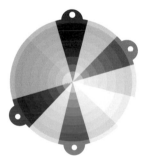

Regal

R 84	R 206	R 92
G 39	G 138	G 160
B 133	B 20	B 56

Retro

R 47	R 241	R 246
G 179	G 86	G 150
B 202	B 79	B 84

Inviting

R 0	R 123	R 206
G 124	G 10	G 128
B 128	B 107	B 20

Playful

R 13	R 208	R 252
G 124	G 63	G 238
B 193	B 65	B 33

Spirited

R 0	R 27	R 138	R 202
G 82	G 125	G 13	G 103
B 149	B 55	B 16	B 32

Healthy

R 103	R 144	R 199	R 192
G 163	G 193	G 77	G 104
B 189	B 62	B 31	B 138

Choosing Your Colors

Before you can decide on a color palette, you need to determine your background color. With the technological advancement of projectors, there are no restrictions on what background color to use anymore, because most colors now translate well. However, in certain circumstances, a darker background might be more effective than a lighter background, and vice versa.

Two factors determine whether dark or light is appropriate: the formality of the event and the venue size. The human eye requires contrast for visibility, and pure black or pure white backgrounds have the greatest opportunity for contrast since they are without color. Look at the color palettes on the right. Here the PowerPoint color palette appears on various colored backgrounds. The palettes on the black and white backgrounds on the opposite page are completely visible and have full contrast. On the midrange colored backgrounds, the contrast is diminished. Some of the colors are indistinguishable from the background, and portions of the palette are unusable.

When choosing your color palette, make sure that it contrasts with the background and the other colors you have chosen—and holds up to a projection test. Colors might look great on your computer screen, but then look different or diluted when projected. If color integrity is important to you, either use your own projector as often as possible or arrive at your venue early enough to have time to adjust the projector.

Dark background

- Formal
- Doesn't influence ambient lighting
- Does not work well for handouts
- Fewer opportunity for shadows
- For large venues
- Objects can glow

Light background

- Informal
- Has a bright feeling
- Illuminates the room
- Works well for handouts
- For smaller venues (conference rooms)
- No opportunity for dramatic lighting or spotlights on the elements

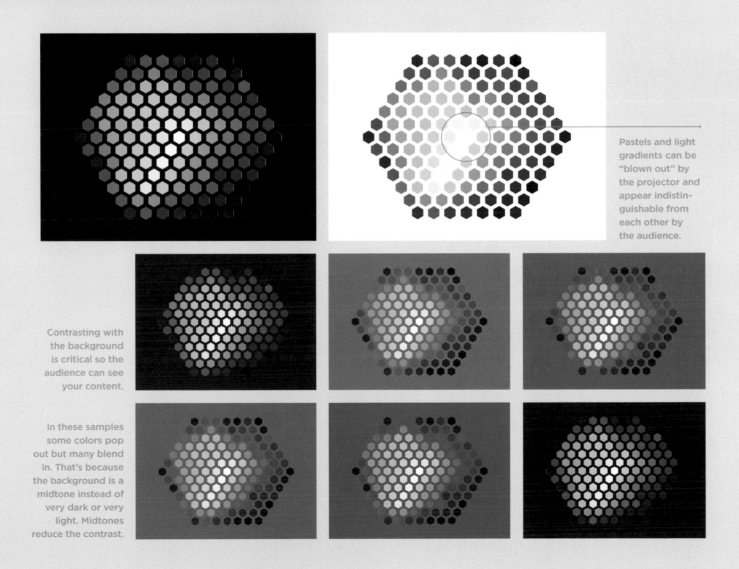

Pastels and light gradients can be "blown out" by the projector and appear indistinguishable from each other by the audience.

Contrasting with the background is critical so the audience can see your content.

In these samples some colors pop out but many blend in. That's because the background is a midtone instead of very dark or very light. Midtones reduce the contrast.

Using Industry Color Palettes

Once you know who your audience is, it's pretty easy to determine what their likes and dislikes are. You can determine which color palette will appeal to the audience by understanding their personality (see bottom of pages 130–131 for various temperaments expressed through color). Colors can also seem masculine or feminine, enticing or reserved.

Another way to pick a palette is to identify colorful images within your industry that can influence your corporate color palette. Identify a series of images that support the subject matter.

Colors were picked directly from the industry photographs.

Agriculture Industry

R 114	R 89	R 250	R 206
G 158	G 149	G 222	G 101
B 60	B 222	B 67	B 54

Contrast is important when choosing your palette because projectors vary and the subtle color differences you set up on your computer screen can get lost. Manually tweak the colors while projecting to ensure they translate well.

The example on the previous page uses images from the agriculture industry. By using a color eyedropper tool, the designer pulled colors directly from the photograph.

Each industry palette can be strikingly unique. This palette built for the automotive industry plays up the metals as the base colors, as well as gold. It doesn't incorporate the paint color of the vehicles themselves. Using gray tones as the primary color palette helps the bright colors pop out against the relatively muted palette.

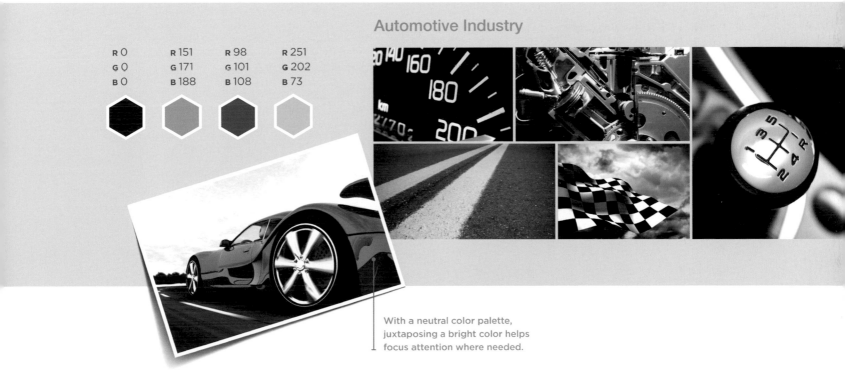

Automotive Industry

R 0
G 0
B 0

R 151
G 171
B 188

R 98
G 101
B 108

R 251
G 202
B 73

With a neutral color palette, juxtaposing a bright color helps focus attention where needed.

Assembling a Color Palette

To assemble a palette, ideally select three to five core colors from the color wheel, plus a neutral and a highlight color. A good place to start is to look at the color(s) of your logo or industry-appropriate colors. Based on the color you select, you can experiment with the various methods of combining and coordinating colors from the previous pages. Also experiment with tint and shade.

Neutral colors often serve as a background element and aid in visual hierarchy and divisions of space. You can use neutrals to create an additional background surface as long as it isn't distracting. For example, white serves as a primary background color for this book while bands of pale gray are sometimes used as a secondary background color to anchor slide samples in the case studies. Neutrals can also be used in data charts and diagrams as secondary information. Using a neutral color for secondary data helps blend information into the background. That helps the emphasized data stand out. Neutrals can be in shades of the corporate logo color or a tint or shade of the background color being used. Highlight colors accentuate text and create emphasis in charts and infographics.

When you've selected a color palette, also select light and dark tones of the color set. These dark and light tones determine the depth of range for gradients. For example, when you create an object that has a gradient fill, the dark range would serve as shading and the light tones as the highlight.

Once you've finalized your palette, place it on a slide and project it to ensure the colors contrast well against each other.

About 1 in 12 people have some sort of color vision deficiency. Be sure to employ varying brightness in color and choose distinguishable shapes to tell your visual story.

Check your slides for contrast before presenting them by converting the file to grayscale and printing it on a black-and-white printer. Anything that's indistinguishable from the background or other components on the slide could be indistinguishable to someone with a color vision deficiency.

The circle above uses various colorized circles to create the number 74. A color-blind person cannot distinguish the orange tones from the green ones. Odds are high they cannot see the number.

How should this affect the color choices you make for a palette which might be seen by lots of people?

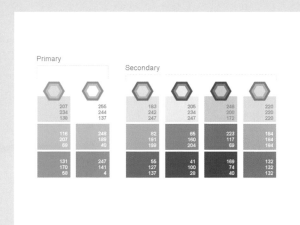

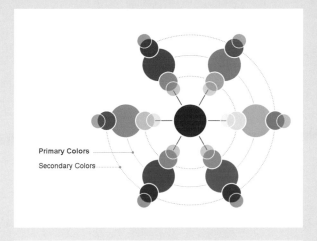

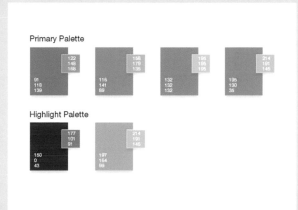

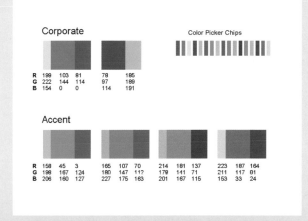

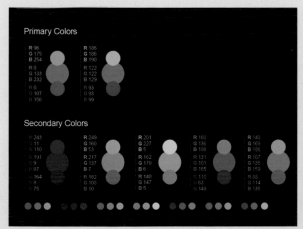

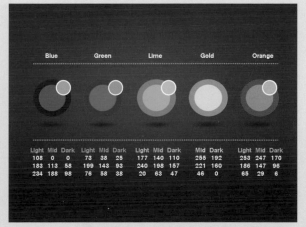

Corporate Overview

BzzAgent

Case Study: BzzAgent
Limiting an Energetic Palette

To harness the power of word-of-mouth marketing, BzzAgent created an infrastructure that enables consumers to share their honest opinions about products. Because their business model relies on attracting people who are brand loyalists as well as energetic communicators, their visual identity—and their color palette specifically—must take a proactive and energetic stance to reflect this.

Take care in selecting images. Have your color palette open while searching for images online. That way you can ensure that the images work well with your palette. Also, when shooting your own photography, have your models wear a wardrobe that complements the color scheme.

For diagrams and illustrations, the designer needed to select additional colors but use them sparingly. The two colors in their existing palette plotted on the wheel as almost an analogous palette because they're so close on the color wheel. We used those colors as a starting point. In an effort to continue to constrain the colors for dramatic appeal, we decided to keep all the colors on one side of the color wheel and select every other color on the wheel (in various shades and tints). We made sure that the new colors played a secondary role to the two colors in the core palette. Beware of visually overwhelming your audience by giving equal value to all colors.

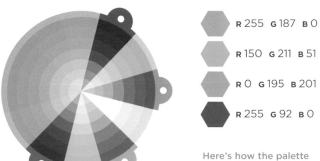

R 255 G 187 B 0

R 150 G 211 B 51

R 0 G 195 B 201

R 255 G 92 B 0

Here's how the palette plots on the color wheel. Selecting colors from one side of the color wheel ensured contrast *and* color harmony.

It's possible, but extremely challenging, to create diagrams in a palette with only two colors. Adding black sparingly helped emphasize important points by increasing the contrast.

Text

Remember the 3-second rule.

Presentations are a "glance media"—more closely related to billboards than other media. It requires commuters to process quickly as they drive past. Imagine having a billboard full of bullets, drivers would crash trying to process the ads.

Ask yourself whether your message can be processed effectively within three seconds. The audience should be able to quickly ascertain the meaning before turning their attention back to the presenter. For comparison, consider that when billboards first appeared, a public outcry ensued over concerns of driver safety and visual pollution of the landscape. Interestingly, relatively few protests have aired against the visual pollution in meeting rooms across corporate America.

Content should lend itself to quick processing, and should be typeset correctly.

When Apple's Macintosh first debuted, anyone with a computer could now be a desktop publisher. At Duarte, we dove in head first and were thrilled when a reputable design firm invited us in for a portfolio review. While reviewing our work, the Creative Director's expressions and line of questions made me squirm. Over and over, she asked probing questions about our typesetting decisions. I could tell she was not impressed. She told us that we needed to master type if we wanted to stand out from all the novices entering the field in droves. We took her advice and studied the masters.

Her advice was timely. Shortly after, we were approached by Adobe and Apple, who both treat type as a critical component to the success of their brands. They took as much care around the treatment of type as they did their concept, copy, images, and layouts. Our accurately type-set presentations helped us land these accounts.

Some might say that typesetting isn't worth the extra time for a presentation. But type is a fundamental part of our culture and has been for centuries. Most people can inherently and easily recognize when type is balanced and used well.

Before computers, typesetting was a specialized skill and honorable profession. Digitization of fonts and the advent of the personal computer spawned a massive generation of users who don't understand the context and beauty in carefully typeset design.

Dissecting a Font

Every font has its own personality: serious or playful, stately or friendly, bold or humble. Here are two different fonts. Study them and look for the obvious and subtle differences. When you've trained yourself to see the differences, you can make better choices about which font is the most appropriate for your presentation.

Consider the height and weight. Look at the various shapes created by the ascenders and descenders. Notice the unique shapes formed in the negative space of the letters, called *counters*. The two words shown here are the same point size, but the x-height is taller in the sans serif font. Choose a font that accurately reflects the personality of your brand—like the examples shown to the right.

There isn't much that turns my stomach more than seeing someone use a foot mark where an apostrophe should be. Make sure your apostrophes have a head and a tail. If they look like splinters it's bad; if they look like tadpoles, it's good.

Serif

Serifs are intended for a long sequence of words that exceed one line. They have little feet that guide the letters into each other so the letters appear connected, and to help the eye stay within the line of text in dense copy. Serifs possess varying line weights that help the eye identify the letter quickly.

Sans Serif

The word "sans" means without, so sans serif means without serifs. The letterforms are bigger and bolder. Sans serif typefaces are usually used in children's books because of their simplicity. Some believe they are more difficult to read, so they are usually used in short bursts like headlines, subtitles, and captions.

Font	Personality
Georgia	formal, practical
Times New Roman	professional, traditional
Courier	plain, nerdy
Arial	stable, conformist
Tahoma	young, plain
Century Gothic	happy, elegant

The debates still rage about which type is most suited for legibility. The results of many studies are inconclusive, so I conducted my own research from the 28th floor of a Las Vegas hotel. If my earlier premise is true that slides are most comparable to billboards, then sans serif is the way to go. Out of the 40 or so billboards visible from the hotel room, the only ones I could read were set in sans serif type. Debate over, I guess.

A fundamental element of design is how the fonts are combined, scaled, tabulated, and spaced.

Just like great wine pairing, font pairing can amplify great design. It is best to combine no more than two fonts per presentation. Use one font for headlines and subheads, and the other for blocks of text.

If you need a special font for emphasis, that might justify a third, but rarely. Instead, use color or italics to create emphasis. More than two fonts will make your slides look busy. Choose your primary typeface wisely and select a secondary font to complement it. It's also perfectly fine to use only one font throughout your presentation.

How Many Words Should Be on a Slide?

There really are no official rules on the word count for a slide. Ultimately, you need enough words to make you comfortable delivering your message. Put enough there to serve as a mnemonic, but go for a very low word count. If you use a plethora of words, your audience will read the slide more quickly than you can explain it, making you strangely irrelevant to your own presentation. One time, for fun, I delivered a presentation by just being quiet and letting my staff read the slides. It was a hoot. We were done at least ten minutes sooner!

The default template in PowerPoint is a slideument. This is not a visual aid; it is a document. Avoid two-line titles when giving a presentation because of the distance the eye has to travel across the slide. In fact, consider doing a presentation with titles only, like the one below.

Simple Works!

- Succinct text
- Crisp thoughts
- Big ideas
- Clear mnemonic
- Relieved audience

The Default Blank Template Accommodates a Two-line Title

- Primary bullet is 32 points, which is good
  - Then return and tab for the second level
    - Notice that the bullet style changes at each level
      - With each new tab the font's point size is reduced
        - The smallest text is 20 points, which is slideument size

- When you move to a second point
  - It becomes obvious that this just might be
    - Something you want t he audience to read
      - Instead of hearing you present the content
        - In compelling and human way

The standard default PowerPoint template above encourages two-line titles and sub, sub, sub, sub, sub points. It's a document, not a slide.

Revealing Text

Now that you've determined how much text is on a slide, you need to decide in what order and how quickly the audience should see the text. I prefer to have text build sequentially as I'm not sure why anyone would want the audience to jump ahead. Remember, if the audience can see your bullets, they know the points you're going to make. They'll get bored or agitated waiting for you to catch up with them.

If you choose to repeat an agenda slide in your presentation to give the audience context, gray out previous text so they can visually jump to the current point.

T!P

Don't animate your text unless it adds value, meaning, or emotion to the content.

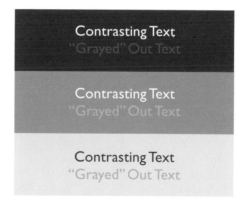

Use a lighter or darker shade of the background color to dim text.

Typesetting

If you plan to use large words by themselves or combine them with an image, take the time to typeset the text.

In the same way that grammar and punctuation errors can distract some of your audience, typographic laziness can irk those with right-brain tendencies. Case in point: Steve Jobs built typesetting features into the very first Mac because he considered his users and had the foresight to see the importance of typesetting. Smart and innovative people do their homework. And these are the people you want as clients. So spend a few moments typesetting. You never know who's in the audience.

Simplicity is powerful.

Type alone can convey messages succinctly. Use a single word or phrase to get your point across. Often, nothing else is needed.

Ligatures

Ligatures occur when two or more letterforms are joined as a single glyph. The most common English combinations usually begin with the letter "f." The word "firefly" has two opportunities for ligatures: "fi" and "fl." In the example to the right, the two individual letters are replaced with a single letterform. The bulb of the "f" combines with the dot in the "i," creating a unique letterform that replaces two characters. Common ligatures are fl, fi, ft, ff, ffl, ffi.

Kerning

Kerning adjusts the space between individual letters. A well-kerned font reduces the amount of visually awkward gaps between letters. Turn auto-kerning on in your presentation software. Common letters that need to be kerned manually are capital letters: A, R, T, V, W, Y.

Look at the word "WAR". It is not kerned. You can see how the slant of the "W" is parallel with the slant on the "A" but there's a large gap between the two letters. Compare this with the slide on the opposite page where the word "WAR" is properly kerned.

Letterspacing

Letterspacing—also called tracking—refers to the amount of space between letters that affects the overall density of a word. The slide on the opposite page with the word "spacious" has loose letterspacing.

Ligatures not used

Gaps and spaces make awkward negative spaces between letters.

BEFORE: Default PC type

AFTER: Ligatures and kerning applied

Final typeset word applied to a slide.

Typesetting a Block of Text

Paragraph spacing determines the gap between blocks of text. In the case of bullet points, each bullet is considered a new paragraph, whereas a second line in a bullet is not.

This is paragraph Spacing!

Can you see that just above this line of text, the space is larger than the type within the paragraph? Line spacing is the space between lines within a paragraph. Holding down the Shift key and then pressing Return (called a soft return) creates line spacing, whereas pressing the Return key alone (called a hard return) will give you paragraph spacing.

Title placed here

- Insert your bullet line
- Insert your bullet line
- Insert your bullet line
- Insert your bullet line

Bullets
Notice the paragraph spacing between each bullet paragraph.

Title placed here

- Major Bullet number 1
  - Sub-bullet number 1
  - Sub-bullet number 2
- Major Bullet number 2
  - Sub-bullet number 1
  - Sub-bullet number 2

Sub-bullets
If you insist on using them, they should be spatially associated with the primary bullet. Notice how there's a larger space between the sub–bullet and next major bullet. That's paragraph spacing.

In typesetting terms, a widow is a single word by itself at the end of a paragraph (in this case it is the word "performs").

"The typographer must analyze and reveal the inner order of the text, as a musician must reveal the inner order of the music he performs."

Robert Bringhurst

The above text is aligned left. The rag is the shape that the text makes on the nonaligned side (in this case the right side). Look at the shape and determine if it has a distracting shape. In this case the word "reveal" sticks out too much, and the word "performs" in the last line is a widow. Usually all can be fixed easily by making a minor adjustment to the width of the text block, making manual line breaks with a soft return, or both.

"The typographer must analyze and reveal the inner order of the text, as a musician must reveal the inner order of the music he performs."

Robert Bringhurst

Adjusting the text box creates a straighter rag and removes the widow.

Obeying Gun Laws and Bullet Laws

Guns don't kill people, as the saying goes, but bullets kill plenty. Many an audience has fallen prey to bullet slide after bullet slide, and a dead audience (even metaphorically speaking) won't help you achieve your presentation objectives!

Protect your audience from the dangers of bullets with a few simple guidelines. First, if you have to use bullets at all, use them sparingly.

Many rules have been written about how many bullets should be on a slide. But, ignore the 4x4 rule, and the 5x5 rule, and the 7-word per slide rule. Instead, use good design sense to visually compose your bullet slides.

T!P
Keep a copy of the *Chicago Manual of Style* and *Words into Type* and refer to them often.

Jerry Weissman, author of *The Power Presenter,* strongly believes that when you create a text slide containing bullets, you are, in effect, presenting headlines only. As the presenter, it's your job to put flesh on the bones of the skeletal bullets. The presenter provides the body text around the headline. When composing your bullets, think of them as newspaper headlines. Keep them as succinct as possible and write each line in parallel structure. That means that each one must begin with the same tense and the same part of speech: verb, noun, adjective, and so on. Whether your first bullet is a sentence or just a fragment, make the rest of them the same. And finally, avoid the extra visual complexity of sub-bullets whenever you can.

Standard convention traditionally uses title case for titles and initial caps (capitalizing only the first word of the line) for everything else. You can't go wrong with this convention. But some companies have other conventions that are dictated by their brand guidelines. Use all caps sparingly and only for emphasis because, as with e-mail, caps can be perceived as shouting.

Whatever you choose, do it consistently. It's bothersome if some bullets have a period and others don't. Likewise, slides that use title case followed by slides employing initial caps are disconcerting. Bullet points, too, should either all be initial cap or use another convention. Remember, consistency is key.

This bullet slide boiled down the contents from this spread into a brief, parallel structure.

Bullet Laws

- Protect audience
- Use sparingly
- Write headlines
- Use parallel structure
- Avoid sub-bullets

Validating Your Font Size

What is the most appropriate minimum font size? If you have to ask, you may be using your slides as a document. Here are a few good approaches:

---

1. Measure the diagonal length of your computer screen. Let's say it's a 21 inch monitor. Using a tape measure, place a piece of tape 21 feet from your screen. If your screen is 17 inches, place the tape 17 feet away, etc. Then, launch a slide on your screen into slide show mode. Whatever you cannot see from behind the piece of tape probably can't be seen by the back of the room.

2. Put your file into slide sorter view. Look at the slides at 66 percent size. If you can still read them, so can your audience.

3. Stand in the back of the room at your venue and click through all the slides so you know what people in the back row will see.

4. Follow the advice of Guy Kawasaki, author and former Apple Fellow: "A good rule of thumb for font size is to divide the oldest investor's age by two, and use that font size."

Playing Text Animations as the Audience Enters

Many times at large venues it's nice to have an animation playing as the attendees fill the room. Often, these "curtain warmers," "splash animations," and "walk-in animations" feature quotes, trivia, factoids, imagery, video, or whatever fits the theme and temperament of your event or presentation. If produced well, these animations can be timed to music and incorporate voice-over audio content as well. They are simple to produce and have just as much impact as a fancy video.

You can also use these animations the way interstitials are used on TV—as mini bites of content that play when filler programming is needed. So at your presentation, when there's a break in the session or a cut to another screen for a demo, these animations fill screen space when the presenter isn't projecting slides.

For a biotech company's sales event, we created a theme graphic that was used throughout the venue and incorporated it into a clean but simple background for a "walk-in" animation.

This simple animation sequence was typeset and animated elegantly. Look at how the "i" in coaching combines with the "l" in excellence. The second "l" in excellence attaches to the dot on the "i" of the word "in." These subtle typesetting decisions defined how the animations were applied.

www

CHAPTER 8

Using Visual Elements: Images

Assembling an Image System

It benefits the entire organization to have a library of images with re-usable parts and pieces that employees can draw on. This way they don't have to scramble to find appropriate industry-related images for their presentation. They'll have access to pre-approved images, which helps productivity by having key design decisions already made. They'll have the tools they need at hand so they can focus on building effective content rather than scrambling to create elements from scratch.

This section focuses on two types of images: photography and illustration.

This chapter covers the fundamentals, as well as stylistic insights that will help guide you in determining the right approach for your images.

JAN • 66 •

A powerful image library creates re-usable components that fit together well with each other. Systems like this enable you to focus on your thinking.

Photography
Establishing a Photographic Family

Take the time to select a family of images that works well together. Your lazy competitors will grab the first image that shows up in an image search, so invest the time to pull together wel-thought-through concepts. Photos should work as a cohesive system, as if the same photographer took them all.

Notice how both columns of photos have the same subject matter, but the second column looks like a family of images. They have similar lighting and color tones.

Consider also the content of your photography. Two hands shaking in front of a globe? A group of nondescript people smiling over a laptop? These situations do not happen in real life. If you want to truly connect with your audience, you must present photography that favors realism over staged or metaphorical approximation.

T!P

Select images of people that:

• Reflect the audience's culture or ethnicity
• Are context-appropriate
• Don't crop their subjects at the neck
• Represent industry, customer experience, and real-life situations
• Account for the current era

Cheesy   **System**

partnership

training

challenges

success

These cheesy images are all different styles...   ...whereas these photos work together well.

The Rule of Thirds

Composing your photos based on a simple grid of thirds is a trick used by movie producers, graphic designers, and professional photographers. Using the rule of thirds leads to aesthetically pleasing and professional-looking imagery.

The rule is applied by dividing your photo into thirds both vertically and horizontally. Don't be afraid to re-compose an existing shot so that key features fall at power points for maximum impact. Believe it or not those crosshairs are called power points. This helps create a composition that is balanced, possesses energy, and creates more interest than simply centering the featured element. The focal point of the image is slightly off-center, which also gives you open space for text on the slide. Many newer digital cameras feature a grid system built-in as an option, so turn it on and align your shots to it. Next time you're watching a movie, look for scenes filmed with the focal point off-center and falling within this grid of thirds. Most scenes will.

○ **power points**

Crop images so they focus on what's most important.

Case Study: School District
Fun with a Focus

Why did most teachers get into education in the first place? It's the kids. So why not make kids the focus of a school district's grand plan to revitalize their approach to education?

Happy kids, bright colors, and simple compositions set a cheerful tone while illustrating the goal of the district's initiative: putting the fun back into education.

The next step for the designers was to visualize the plan and make a diagram graphic that would most effectively communicate the plan. The final graphic depicts students at the center of the educational process to remind everyone that kids should be the focus of education, that everything should revolve around them and their needs.

This concentric diagram is layered (page 49) and serves as the touchstone of the presentation. Representing students with the green dot at the center, teachers visualize how the new initiatives revolved around their charges.

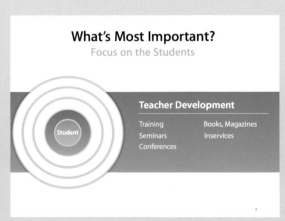

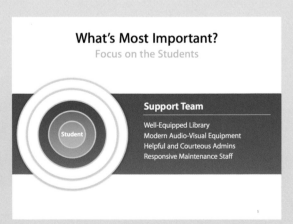

Using duotone photographs of energized students as color-coded transition slides reinforced the district's positive message and reminded teachers of why they became educators in the first place.

Together, the photography and the information design appealed to teachers, administrators, and district officials on both intellectual and emotional levels.

Taking Your Own Photos

Many times the best photo to tell your story doesn't exist at any of the online photo houses. Take custom photos to help drive the message home. Think outside the box. Don't start off by searching for existing photos. Instead, think about what type of picture would tell your story most effectively, and shoot or find that specific image. Make sure that you carefully light your subjects and avoid any awkward shadows. Extra planning will save you time by eliminating the need to manipulate the photo digitally afterward.

To explain Mozilla's truly open source solution, the metaphor of pre-set Lego kit was used. The kit was prepackaged as a pirate ship, it won't make a very good house, spaceship, or dinosaur. But Mozilla's solution isn't a pre-made kit; its open source has no restrictions.

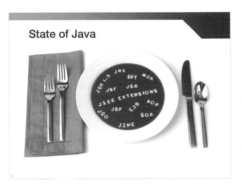

State of Java

After buying a can
of alphabet soup,
the letters were
pulled out and
carefully placed
on top of a bowl
of tomato soup.

T!P
Own your images. Do not
snag images from the Web.
If your presentation becomes
popular online, the owner
of the images can insist you
pay usage rights. That can
be expensive.

These pie slices were used to
explain how the U.S. healthcare
system is fragmented and discon-
nected. The various powers and
special interest groups are keeping it fragmented to preserve
their own piece of the pie.

Illustrations
Using the Personality of Lines

Lines play an important role in illustrations. They are the foundation of an illustration. There are many widths, types, and textures to a line, and each displays a different temperament. Straight lines with sharp corners have a more direct and analytical feel to them, whereas a curvy line is more playful and casual. Choose lines that support the rest of your design. You can also develop an overall system for the lines where various line styles are used for different purposes within the presentation. Whatever decisions you make, be consistent throughout.

Line Width

¼ pt	
½ pt	
¾ pt	
1 ½ pt	
2 ¼ pt	
3 pt	
4 ½ pt	
6 pt	

The thinnest lines are tough to project and might not show up when projected in a large venue.

Line Type

dotted	
dashed	
zig-zag	
curved	
freeform	

Line Texture

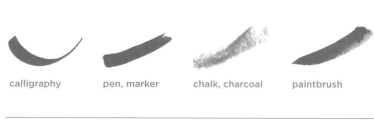

calligraphy   pen, marker   chalk, charcoal   paintbrush

To create textured lines, you have to either use an application other than your presentation software or draw them by hand and scan them in like the samples above.

To create this hand-drawn overlay, print out a photo and place tracing paper over it. Hand-draw or paint new elements into the scenes. Scan in the sketches, make the image background transparent, and place them on top of the photo. You can even animate them. (For example, the swing on the tree moves in the above example).

Creating an Illustration Library

Either buy pre-illustrated icons or hire an illustrator to create a custom robust library of icons that are relevant to your industry. All the graphics on this page were created in an isometric style. They have no vanishing point, which makes all the sides of the illustrations parallel to the opposite side. This illustration method makes it easy for anyone to assemble the graphics because they will all appear to be sitting on the same surface no matter where you put them.

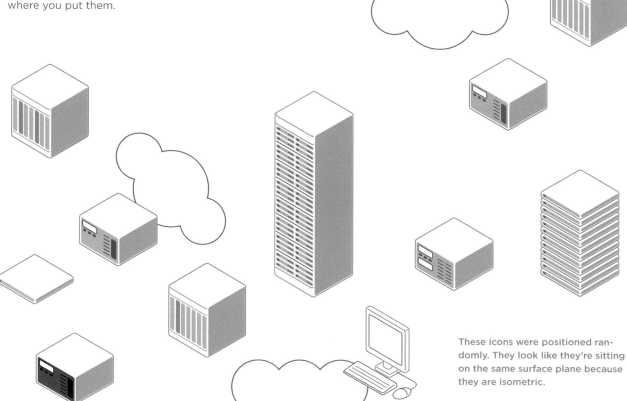

These icons were positioned randomly. They look like they're sitting on the same surface plane because they are isometric.

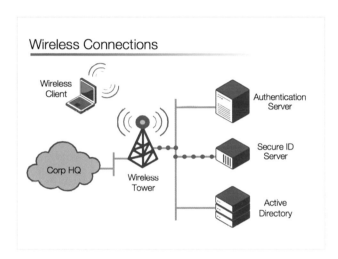

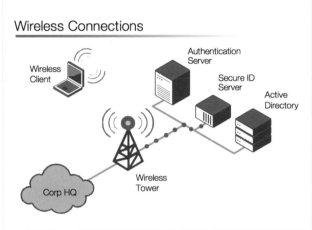

Notice how the isometric icons in these two samples can be connected with horizontal or diagonal lines and still look right. These isometric illustrations provide enormous flexibility when it comes to arrangement.

T!P

If you're pioneering an industry, one way to establish dominance is to invest in an art library and then give it away to your entire industry, including your competitors.

Since its inception, Cisco has given away its art library. The company wanted its own representations of a network to be the industry standard.

Illustrating Complex Stories

Sometimes the concepts to be communicated are complex. It's not a simple task to represent the intricacies of high tech, business, or biotech processes. Such complex diagrams are often called infographics and have a depth of information.

Each of these illustrations is a system that shows how things work. It's best to build and animate these complex stories so the audience understands the interconnectedness of the various parts over time.

When illustrations get too complex, it is best to bring in a professional illustrator. Here are some pointers for working with one.

Virus Attack

Successful Handoff
It's best to tell the illustrators the "story" that you want to say instead of telling them what to draw. This lets them propose a solution from a fresh perspective that's easily digestible for your audience.

Give Them Time
A complex illustration often requires research, ideation, and cycles of revision. All three take time. If you are time-strapped and have a clear vision for the final product, then draw a sketch. It could save time and money.

Let Them Be Experts
They really do know what works. Listen to them carefully, and trust their input. Untrained and subjective opinions can derail the outcome of a project.

Be Decisive
Give clear, objective feedback including that of all stake holders, but consolidate it into clear non-conflicting directions.

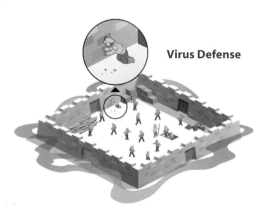

Virus Defense

In this pair of illustrations, a computer virus attacked a kingdom and infected the citizens of the fortified city. The bottom illustration shows the IT professional (dressed as a guard) plugging the hole where the virus entered.

www

Making a complex commerce transaction look simple isn't easy. Placing buyers on one end and suppliers on the other, you can see in general terms how the systems connect and give real-time data to both.

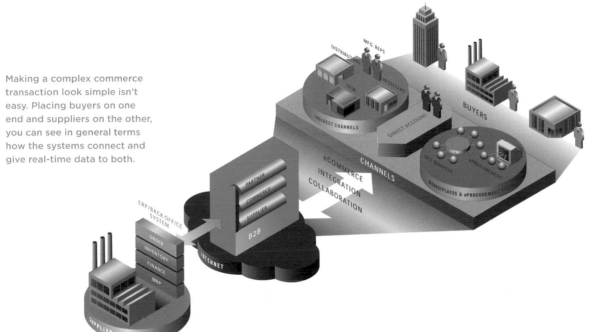

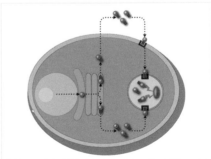

©Betsy Palay, Hyseq Pharmaceuticals, Inc.

Turning bioinformation into biotherapeutics: A proprietary biotechnology screening process uses a large database to identify human gene sequences that may be useful in creating new medicines.

©Betsy Palay, Transkaryotic Therapies, Inc.

Protein development platform: A human cell synthesizes, transports, and replaces important protein molecules. This pathway may lead to the development of medicines that treat patients suffering from rare genetic diseases.

Stylizing Diagrams and Illustrations

On the right hand page is a collection of stylized diagrams. The root shape is the same, but the scale, surface, lighting, and texture differ for each one. Each diagram has its own personality. The diagrams would look ridiculous if they were put into the same presentation file together.

Now that presentation applications have built-in 3D capability and lighting effects, be aware of choosing styles that work well together in the same scene.

Making Diagrams Consistent

Standardize on one texture, light source, or pattern unless the concept you're communicating needs more. Do not use clip art, ever. Hire a local illustrator to build a set of key images that you can use that map to your story.

Buying illustrations online is priced reasonably, but select illustrations and diagrams that look like they were all created by the same illustrator.

T!P

Hold down the Shift key to scale images and objects while preserving their original proportions.

This is the original diagram that has been stylized several different ways.

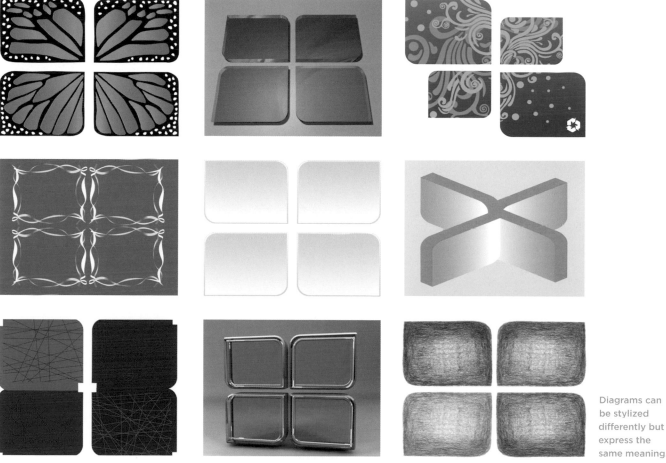

Diagrams can be stylized differently but express the same meaning.

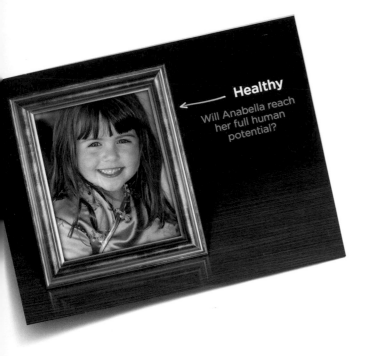

Case Study: Dr. Mike Magee
Home Is Where Our Health Is

More and more, healthcare is emerging as a central concern. And Dr. Mike Magee, author of *Home-Centered Health Care,* believes that preventative measures and detailed future-planning are critical to a sustainable system. But here's where his philosophy departs from other models. Rather than focus on patients and their illnesses—or lack thereof—Dr. Magee emphasizes the home as a specific geographic location where nutrition, exercise, education, and safety all contribute to a healthy present and future.

The challenge therefore, lies in visually distinguishing the presentation as far from a cold, sterile hospital environment as possible, instead bringing the audience into the warm, comforting environment of a home.

Dr. Magee has high expectations for his presentations because his messages impact so many people. He does a great job combining strong visuals with moving stories, pertinent data, and innovative solutions that could solve our health crisis.

Each section of the presentation designed for Dr. Magee uses textures found in the home, like wood grain, fabric, and leather. Hand-drawn illustrations imbue the presentation with a tactile, home-made feel, almost as if a marker had been used to draw icons and infographics directly on the backgrounds. And photos are treated the way you'd see them displayed in your grandparents' home: elegantly framed and positioned prominently as to say, "This is what's important in my life."

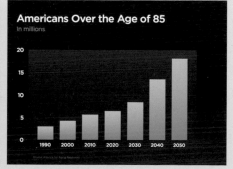

Packed with real stories from Dr. Magee's own life, this presentation describes how his family has had to cope with health issues. Simple yet powerful imagery tells the story of how his father-in-law died at the age of 44, leaving behind ten children and a wife.

A subtle gradient behind the charts increases the contrast. The colors also contrast well with the background.

Case Study: Incorporating Video
Presentation as Punishment

As a parent, there isn't much scarier than watching teenagers push the boundaries too far. So when Duarte VP Dan Post had one too many dangerous close calls with his two sons, he had the perfect consequences. They would spend a Saturday morning developing a presentation about boundaries. Dan started with the seed of an idea. They brainstormed, planned, filmed, and produced this presentation in Apple's Keynote in under four hours.

Integrating video into a presentation seems intimidating, but it's not as much about the quality of the production as it is the creativity of the idea. It needs to be produced at a high enough quality to get the point across, but doesn't require elaborate staging. We call these "video slides." Incorporating short motion clips can have a powerful—and unexpected—impact. Each video lasts from a few seconds to a half minute and can help get more complex points across quite economically.

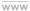

They taped down the feet of a Ken doll and placed firecrackers in the hollow of his back. It couldn't have turned out better if Hollywood had produced it. The little denim jeans remained swaying alone as the debris (and a head) fell to the surface with a small clattering noise, followed by shocking silence. After peals of roaring laughter, the guys got Dad's point. They didn't need to receive the presentation, having internalized the message in the course of building it.

Bungee Cord Parenting
Dad 3.0

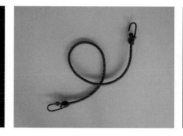

"To know a boundary is also to be aware of what it bounds, and what lies beyond it."

Philosophy 101: Hegel, Kant and Dad

Why?

Things seem a little **foggy**...

You haven't done the best job of self-regulating lately.

You must view the edge without going to jail or dying.

Going **b e y o n d** and **coming back**

You've been damn **lucky**

Experience will lead to better **judgement**.

Until then...

Connected freedom.

CHAPTER 9

Creating Movement

Designing Time-Based Scenes

When things move, the eye is drawn to them like a moth to light. It's unavoidable. Humans are hard-wired to look when things move, primarily from the innate fight-or-flight instinct. They will process what moves and make sure they're not in danger.

Unfortunately, when the software was designed, the developers did not anticipate these instinctual characteristics. If animation is incorporated without purpose or meaning, the audience's attention is turned away from the presenter and toward the movement. It's inevitable.

Presentations are almost the only time-based media that professionals use on a daily basis. It's tempting to make everything buzz like a fly or swoosh like a rocket. Don't do it.

Every change, no matter how subtle, creates distraction. Every animation, no matter how well-intended, affects an audience's ability to grasp insights. And that's not to say animations are a bad thing; they should be used only to help an audience process information. But for some reason, many presenters struggle with selecting animation wisely.

As a presenter, you might quickly recognize the opportunity to design content effectively. But you also need to think about designing—intentionally—the time-based elements within a presentation. Animation is not last-minute icing on the cake; it's a key communication strategy.

Planning Animations

According to the book of Ecclesiastes, "There's a time to live and a time to die." The same is true for animations: There is a time for them to live, and there's a time for them to just NOT!

If you choose to use animation, it should look natural and alive.

The word animation is derived from the Latin word *anima*, which loosely means "the breath of life." Most presentation animation sucks the life out of the audience instead of breathing life into it.

The movement of objects should seem familiar and make sense.

Animation should help you understand the interrelatedness or sequence of information you're presenting. The audience should be able to process the information in the order that the animation presents it.

Because of the important role motion plays in a story, Hollywood painstakingly plans every scene and movement. Storyboards detail each scene change and each move the actor makes is extensively planned.

In presentations, the actors are your elements, and each needs to serve in helping tell your story better. You may not need to create elaborate storyboards, but you should identify the places where animation will help get your point across, and invest planning, thinking, and time into making it powerful.

Make sure that you're synchronized with your slides. By nature, viewers will read and process the visual information the moment it's presented. This can create confusion when a slide has several visuals, but the speaker is expounding on only one. The audience will try to listen while reading ahead at the same time.

Hide elements until you need to refer to them. This ensures the item being discussed will remain the focus of your audience—resulting in the audience listening more and reading less. Which is the point of having a speaker in the first place.

T!P

Slow moving animation (the Ken Burns type) can help create a feeling of nostalgia or even the passage of time.

Fast-moving animation (quick cuts) can help create a sense of excitement, energy, or surprise.

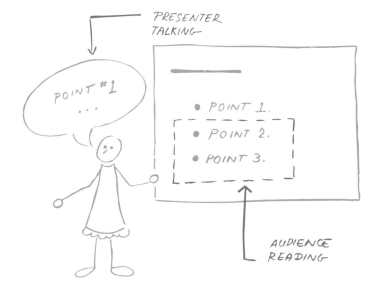

Animating Serves a Purpose

When assembling a slide, pretend you're a movie director looking through a camera lens.

The film director is responsible for overseeing every creative aspect of a film, including how it should look, what tone it should have, and what an audience should gain from the cinematic experience.

Just like actors, elements can enter a scene, interact, and then leave the scene. There can also be entire scene changes. Animation can show cause and effect with any type of graphical element: color, text, images, diagrams, shapes, lines, etc. Anything can become the actor in your scene.

www

This series of pictures represents how IT professionals are under tremendous pressure. It looks like his cubicle is closing in on him.

Animation uses motion, speed, and direction for these purposes:

Change in Relationship
Change proximity, modify hierarchy, show flow, compare, separate or include, influence or impact, attract or repel

Direction
Enter or exit, zoom in or out, show new viewpoint, pan image or scene, cover or uncover, construct or deconstruct

Change in Object
Morph, modify, vary, scale up or down, simplify or show complexity

Sequence
Transition between scenes, time lapse, grow or decay, process or how-to, pattern emergence

Emphasis
Control eye movement, create contrast, move forward or backward, highlight

Taking Lessons from the Movies

So, if you've decided that animation will help convey your message, you can learn some lessons from the movies. Interestingly, now that presentation applications incorporate animation and video, you are, in a way, sitting in the director's chair.

Over the last hundred years movies have relied on visual language to tell stories and evoke audience emotion. For a crash course in the principles of film language, take a look at Jennifer Van Sijll's best-selling book, *Cinematic Storytelling*. In it she says, "cinematic storytelling is the difference between documenting and dramatizing, between employing the potent storytelling tools in the medium or leaving them silent." That same insight applies to presentations. You can create either a document or a dramatization. Many of the cinematic techniques in Van Sijll's book will inspire you to approach presentations more like a screenwriter than a speechwriter.

A screenwriter's ability to envision the story is what differentiates them from other writers. Successful presentation developers not only focus on the content but should be fluent in conveying what the audience sees on the screen.

Van Sijll's insights into how the "dynamics of the frame" affect movie goers applies to presentations. Here is her fascinating take on how screen direction can impact audiences and contribute to the story.

x-axis

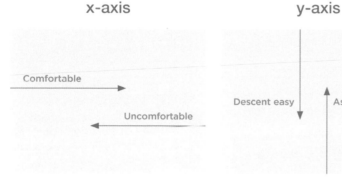

The eye is comfortable moving left to right because it mimics reading. The eye is less experienced moving the opposite direction and is thus less comfortable. In the movies there's a good chance that the "good guy" will enter from the left every time. Conversely, the antagonist usually enters from the right. This subtle irritant directs audiences to see the character negatively.

y-axis

A downward moving object is sensible because of the law of gravity; it is natural for things to descend. Conversely, an upward moving object seemingly resists gravity and is therefore illogical.

Once a downward motion starts, it's hard to stop without the object landing on, or colliding with something.

difficulty of movement

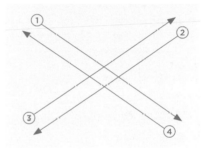

1 Easier
2 Easy
3 Hard
4 Harder

Gravity aids the motion of descending diagonals. The descent seems easy. The left-to-right seems like an easier descent because it follows the direction of reading.

Gravity works against the ascending diagonals. It's easier for an object to fall downward than move upward. The right-to-left ascent is the most difficult of all screen directions because it is counter-intuitive to the reading eye and works against gravity as well.

Making Objects Move and Change

Animation creates the illusion of movement. Presentation software can be used to create an illusion of two-dimensional (and even three-dimensional) animation.

The decisions you make while animating objects influence how quickly the audience can process the information but just as importantly, how much the audience has to move their eyes to process the information. Text dropping down and then bouncing into place is bothersome and not meaningful. Plan out what pacing makes sense,

where objects will travel, and where the object is at in the space. Sometimes using more than one animation feature helps convey a story better.

In the samples below, objects animate to perform a specific action. The action (as well as other potentially perceived meanings) is followed by a representation of how it looks on your slide, and then the actual animation command as found in PowerPoint.

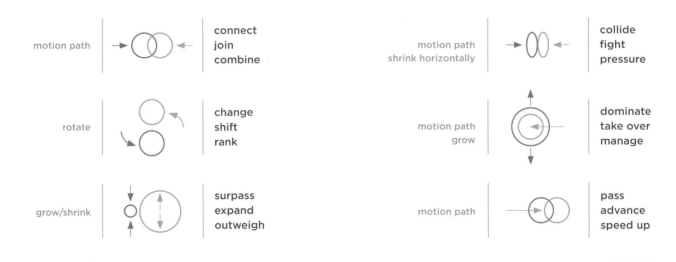

motion path	**connect** / **join** / **combine**
rotate	**change** / **shift** / **rank**
grow/shrink	**surpass** / **expand** / **outweigh**
motion path / shrink horizontally	**collide** / **fight** / **pressure**
motion path / grow	**dominate** / **take over** / **manage**
motion path	**pass** / **advance** / **speed up**

www

To make them look natural, you need to create the following animation examples using more than one animation effect in your application. The circle is modified into an oval in the second frame, showing the influence that the impact had on the shape.

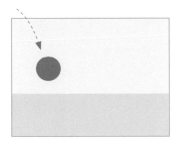

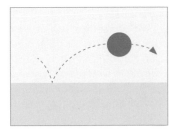

As the object descends, it should move to the right to follow the angle of entry.

Impact of ground contact on the object changes the shape of the object.

The shape is restored; height of the arc is shorter on exit due to energy lost from impact.

When objects enter or exit from a distance, you should apply a path-based animation and scaling effect to the same object. To create the illusion of a third dimension, create a horizon and vanishing point on your slide. For example, this looks like a two-way street.

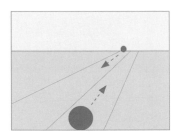
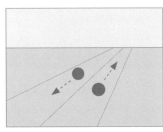
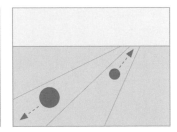

The ball in the foreground is large and the one on the horizon is small. They are entering the scene from two different positions. The balls shrink or grow as they move between the background and foreground.

Creating Panoramas and Scenes

Content can pan from scene to scene, rather than just from slide to slide.

There are times when one slide isn't enough real estate for all your content. Instead of piling it all on one slide, split the content between two slides. You can usually connect them to each other with the push transition in PowerPoint. It will create an illusion that the content is all in the same scene. A transition that makes the slides feel like one large space will help the audience feel like the information is connected within that space.

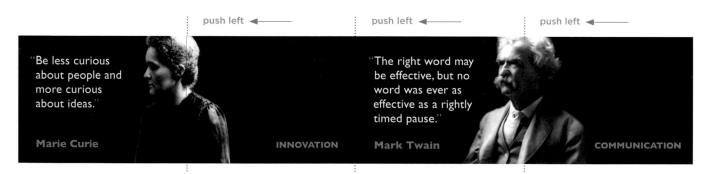

push left ◄——   push left ◄——   push left ◄——

"Be less curious about people and more curious about ideas."

Marie Curie   INNOVATION

"The right word may be effective, but no word was ever as effective as a rightly timed pause."

Mark Twain   COMMUNICATION

Using the push transition in PowerPoint can create the illusion that the camera is panning. In the sample above, it looks like the camera panned to the right across the images and text.

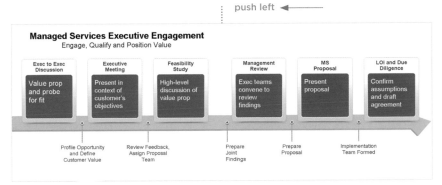

BEFORE: Displayed all at once instead of over time, content is illegible. The audience will read ahead.

AFTER: Complex timeline is split into a sequence of slides. When pushed left with a transition, the presentation gives the illusion of one long timeline.

Have an object enter your slide using a motion path.

Reveal unexpected surprises in the final frame.

Creating Scenes, Not Slides

Think through your presentation as a movie that moves from scene to scene instead as individual snapshots that progress one at a time.

This sample is made up of ten slides. When viewed in a slide show, the slides give you the impression of moving through one long continuous scene. The numbered slides show the sequence of what appears onscreen, along with the PowerPoint transition used for each click.

T!P

If you plan to use this technique, use a template with the sides, top, and bottom free from all ornamentation (page numbers, titles and other standard template elements, or other graphical ornamentation). This way, when the slide is panning through the push transition it does not carry with it a bunch of artifacts from the template.

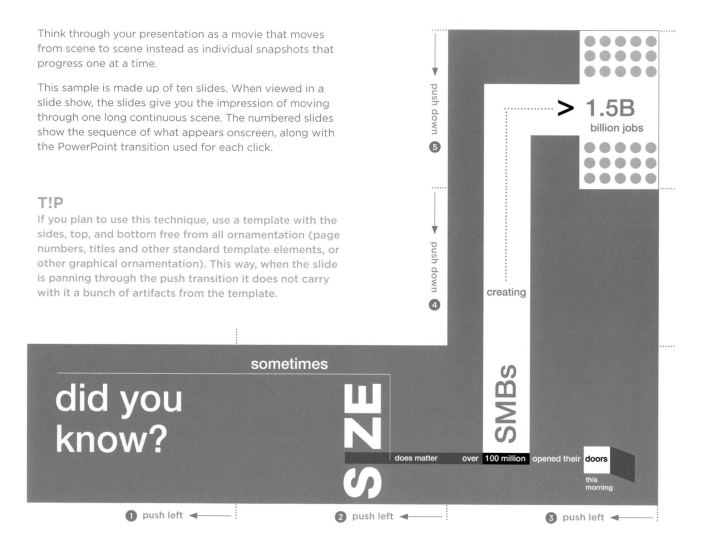

push down ⑤

push down ④

> 1.5B
billion jobs

creating

SMBs

SIZE

sometimes

did you know?

does matter   over 100 million opened their doors

this morning

① push left   ② push left   ③ push left

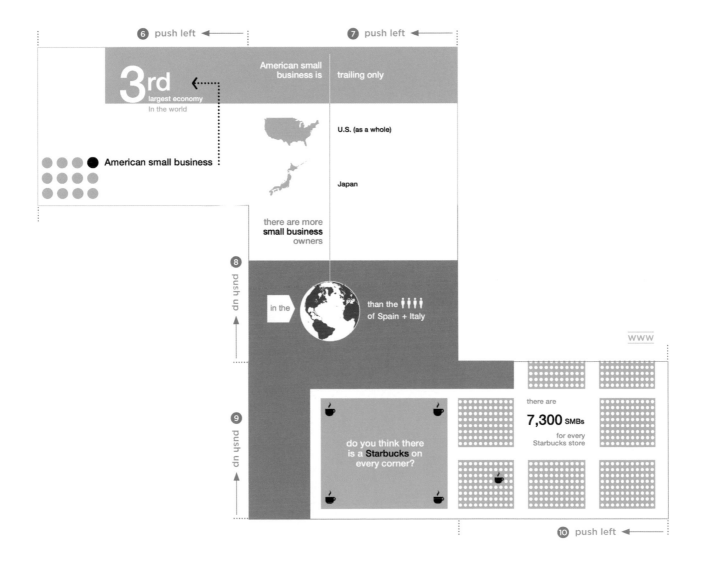

Case Study: Guerrino De Luca
More Than the Sum of Its Parts

It's one thing to retrace the history of home electronics. It's quite another to build the case that navigating this technology is about to get easier—especially with the proliferation of components and their attendant controls. Yet this is the vision that Guerrino De Luca, the CEO of Logitech, set out to communicate at IFA Berlin.

"To explain the new generation of consumer electronics for the digital home, we needed to convey how using brilliant technology can provide a simple, 'technology-free' experience. To illustrate that, I needed to put technology in an historical context," says De Luca. To that end, his presentation followed a path detailing the evolution of home entertainment. At the conclusion of the narrative, which used animated lines to transition between scenes, the perspective pulled back to reveal the bigger picture: a human silhouette.

"The human is at the center of our mission to tame the complexity of entertainment systems in the home."

Guerrino De Luca

The animation also allowed De Luca flexibility in his presentation. Already a powerful speaker, De Luca got the freedom to tell his story without being forced to address every item on a typical bullet-point slide, thanks to the all-graphics, no-words approach.

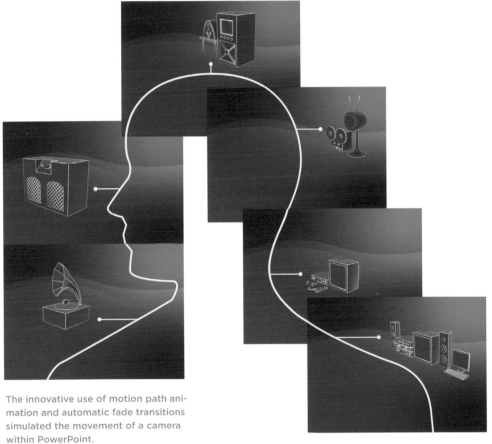

Presenting new products and describing their functions through the use of photos and highlight colors provided a way to communicate the products' usefulness and benefits without becoming bogged down in technical details.

The innovative use of motion path animation and automatic fade transitions simulated the movement of a camera within PowerPoint.

Brainstorming Meaningful Metaphors

Collaborating with others almost always yields a stronger result. After brainstorming at the whiteboard with an executive, we developed a fresh concept to demonstrate Citrix's SmartAccess product. A combination lock serves as a metaphor: the dial spins to create the illusion of granting access.

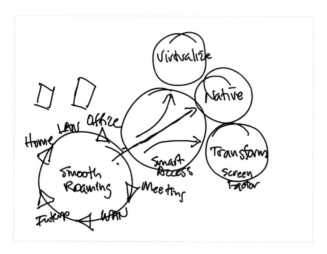

Whiteboard sketch

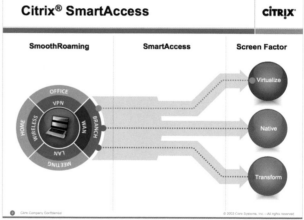

Final illustrated concept

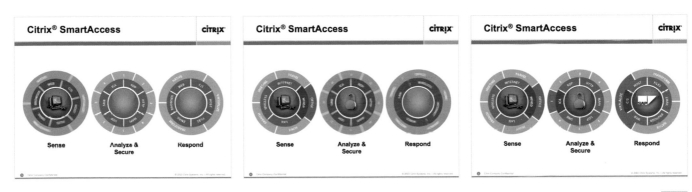

Each dial turns and locks in. This triggers the next dial until all three dials visually look as if they have access to applications.

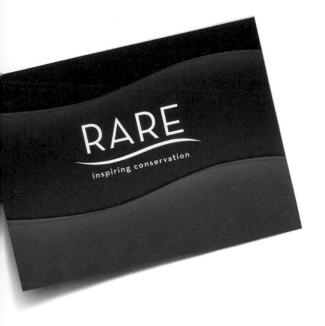

Case Study: Rare
All the World's a Stage

Rare, a U.S.-based conservation organization, works globally to equip people with the tools and motivation they need to raise awareness about, and in turn protect, the vital natural resources in the world's most threatened areas. Rare's strategy uses localized, culturally relevant means to get the message out. They create mascots, use local media, and employ various integrated marketing pieces like posters and bumper stickers to reach and educate all ages in the target community. In trying to stick with the spirit of Rare's mission, a presentation was designed that aligned with their grassroots approach to conservation. We even incorporated our own version of a puppet show: rather than stating the steps needed to become a Rare Champion, we told a story that showed a journey—complete with cast members entering and leaving the "stage." The result illustrates a process that can be replicated worldwide.

The bottom of each slide highlights the current chapter of the story. It shows the entire process starting with the moment a threat to the environment is identified, the several training and planning steps required, and the ultimate goal of engaging many community members to work together to reduce the threat.

WWW

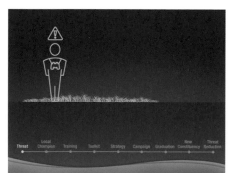

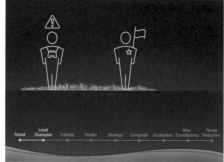

1. A community conservationist identifies a potential threat to the environment.

2. The conservationist contacts Rare, and together they identify a local "champion" to lead a campaign.

3. The champion is sent to one of several universities for specialized training.

4. The champion returns to the community armed with the tools necessary to begin a "pride" campaign.

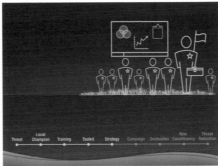

5. The champion meets with local activists to develop and deploy effective strategies.

6. The champion travels to communities, raising awareness and gaining support.

7. The champion graduates from the university program only after proving a successful campaign.

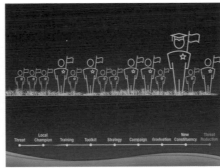

8. The champion continues to gain support even after graduation.

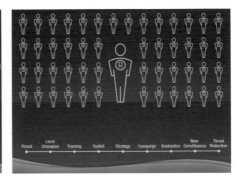

9. The process is complete, the threat is averted, and a community has a new sense of pride in its environment.

Avoiding Visual Vertigo

I recently attended a presentation at a swanky executive briefing center in India. They'd invested big bucks in an animated corporate overview showcased in a plush room that looked like the bridge of the Starship Enterprise. Of the 20 executives in the room, two of them became so motion sick that they sat through most of the presentation with their eyes closed. That's ten percent of the audience lost due to an overzealous animator.

Just because an animation feature is in an application doesn't mean you have to use it.

For many of the companies Duarte works for, we will ban specific animations from their use because they are counter-cultural to the brand personality of that company. It's tough to find a good use for many of the custom animation features in PowerPoint. You need to pretend they aren't there.

You Know You're Using Animation Wrong When

1. The animation is unnatural or counterintuitive.
2. The pace is frenetic, annoying, or chronic (buzzes like a fly).
3. It doesn't add value to the content or serve a purpose.
4. The movement distracts the audience from the presenter.
5. The animation feature is used "just because."
6. Too many animations confuse the purpose.
7. The animation style is inappropriate for the content.
8. A sudden animation surprises or startles the audience.

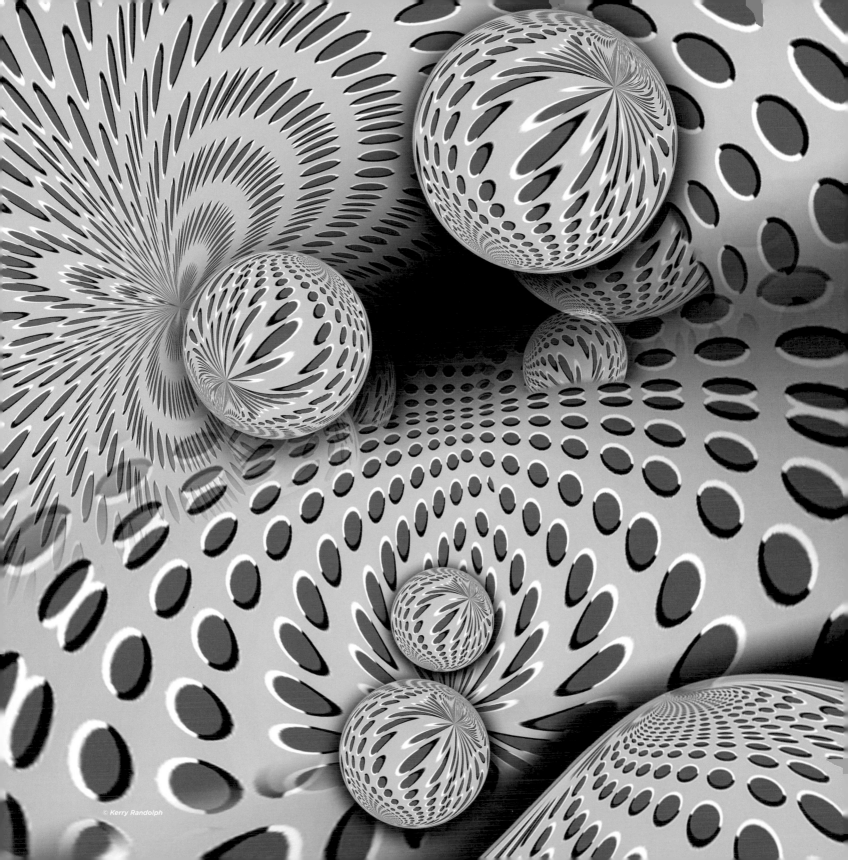

© Kerry Randolph

CHAPTER 10

Governing with Templates

Arming Your Workforce

When more than one person generates presentations for an organization, a well-built template system is a must.

Templates increase employee productivity, constrain exploration, and protect the investment you've made in your brand. You want your clients to have the same visceral reaction to your presentation that they have to your products, services, and ad campaigns. Unfortunately, it's usually tough for the employees building the slides to pull that off. But, by developing a well-designed system of components that employees can build on, you greatly reduce the need for sophisticated skills.

Additionally, most organizations benefit from centralizing design decisions with a few individuals, and then distributing (and rationalizing) those decisions in the template guidelines.

Developing a set of guidelines not only ensures the preservation of the visual attributes of your brand, it streamlines the development process. Because so many people in an organization express the brand in a presentation every day, constraining their design decisions is good. And in a pinch—say, the night before—when you have to Frankenstein a deck together at the last minute, at least the slides will look cohesive. (Whoops, you didn't just read that; never start the night before.)

Always remember, employees are ambassadors of the brand. Their interactions with the industry, clients, and shareholders keep the brand perpetually visible. Arming them with the right tools helps tell a cohesive visual story and also streamlines their presentation development process.

Employees contribute
to the impression your
brand leaves. Arm them
with a good template
to steward it well.

Making Template Design Decisions

Build a template that is timeless so that you won't tire of it easily. If built well, it can remain in circulation for years.

When a large company transitions to a new template, the process can take a Herculean effort that tanks productivity, at least temporarily. The best way to avoid having to re-create the template every time there's an inspiring new ad campaign or marketing whim is to focus on the timeless components of your brand or industry. Those elements are the visual attributes of the brand that rarely, if ever, change. At right are the brand attributes that evolve versus those that remain relatively unchanged. Don't make design decisions that will expire in the short term, or base your decisions on a short-term campaign.

Look through all the material that your company produces and identify the elements that are purely decorative versus those that are the truly essential visual brand elements. For the template, use the essential elements only.

Remember, the template is just that, a template. It should be a basic shell for your words and images. It shouldn't be a stand-alone work of art.

Rarely Change

1. Logo
2. Signage
3. Template-driven systems
   Business systems (letterhead)
   Website framework
   Brochure templates
   Datasheets
4. Visual attributes
   Color palettes
   Grid layouts
   Fonts
   Graphical elements

Often Transform

1. Ad campaigns
2. Marketing campaigns
3. Retail displays and packaging
4. Annual reports

You need to determine what should go in a template, compared to what should go on the slide. To do that, you'll need to identify the varying types of content that your company uses to convey its messages. One approach is to collect files from many departments, audit them, determine communication patterns, and then build a template that meets the communication needs of each organization appropriately.

The effective use of a template helps viewers become accustomed to where the content will appear on a slide and give them a sense that slide content is structured and aligned. Content should not bounce from slide to slide. There's nothing more frustrating than having content jump around so much that each slide becomes a puzzle that takes some study to figure out where to start processing information. Titles and bullet copy should appear in the same locations (unless you've intentionally designed it that way to serve a purpose). By setting the placement and divisions of space for your corporate power-users, they will be able to recognize (and value) the underlying skeletal structure, the reasoning used to develop the template, and the rationale for them to use the template.

T!P

Believe it or not, before you start developing a template, a conversation with your IT department is in order.

- Ask the IT department what the migration plan is for the company's presentation application. If the company is close to a major upgrade, get that beta and begin a strategy on how to build a template in the newest release of the application.

- If you create a template loaded with images, query the IT department whether the organization has adequate storage. Presentation files procreate like bunnies, and a 1MB template might seem innocent, but it can add up to terabytes in a single department in a month.

Case Study: Hewlett-Packard
Branding as a System

One of the few organizations committed to empowering its employees as true ambassadors of the brand, Hewlett-Packard recognized early the prevalence of presentations as a communication medium and worked to ensure that its templates and assets reflected its identity.

HP's success with this initiative stems from the investment the company made in communicating the logic and reasoning behind the system to its employees. In addition to a comprehensive set of slide layouts, an extensive set of guidelines serves as both a training tool and reference for tens of thousands of people. The reasoning is simple: once employees understand the logic behind design decisions, they are more likely to consistently and accurately express the brand.

Title Slide

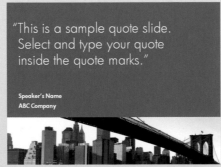

Quote Slide

Transition Slide

Sample of slide types from HP template

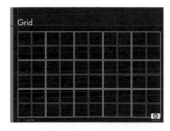

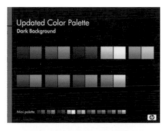

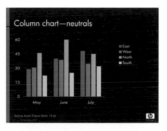

The reusable nature of templates ensures HP's brand is expressed consistently.

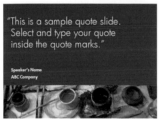

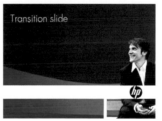

HP's presentation system relies heavily on a set of templates, a flexible color palette, and a dazzling asset library. The carefully culled photography included in the asset library reinforces the HP brand perception, while the use of a strong grid results in consistent layouts. Additionally, the availability of both white and dark blue templates ensures that whether a presentation is delivered to a large audience in a formal setting, or printed and distributed ad hoc, HP's identity always shines through.

The asset library includes a carefully selected, massive collection of industry-specific images to appeal to a range of vertical markets.

Experimenting with Various Looks

When designing a template, start with the branded walk-in and transition screens first. A branded walk-in screen is the visual that's displayed while the audience enters the room and will be the first impression they have of you. So don't just go with the first and most obvious design decisions. Explore a bit to make sure it's just right.

The sets of images shown here are samples of a predominantly red-and-black template. Each design is unique but meets the criteria of being a red-and-black template. Each set of slides has a distinct look that projects very different visual tones. Once you choose the final design, use that as a building block for the template. For example, if you were to choose the design to the right the template pages would most likely incorporate the ribbon as a texture in some way.

Each of these template designs has a different personality and photo style.

Following Template Guidelines

It's possible to develop unlimited masters or "content holders" when building a template. But it's also necessary to provide the logic behind the design decisions and how they support the overall brand. Template guidelines can be as short as five slides or as comprehensive as 150 slides. Once you've determined how your organization uses presentations to communicate, be sure to include a visual representation of the design decisions chosen for each form of content.

For example, if your organization communicates heavily using diagrams, your template might contain several pages of diagrams. Or, if you're a financial institution, many types and styles of charts might be appropriate. If you have a beautiful consumer product with amazing photography, then showcasing how the images should be used over several template slides would be in order. If you're an engineering–driven organization, it might be most important to have Gantt charts, clear timelines, and product roadmaps. You get the drift. Build a template that suits the way your organization communicates.

Segue

Branded slide during walk-in

Title slide

Transition slide

These visuals are just one representation of typical layout types. Your organization might need multiples of each layout.

Q&A
(branded walk-out)

Content

Text slide

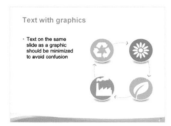

Text with graphic

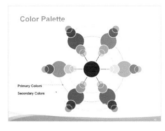

Quote slide

Charts and tables

Components

Grid

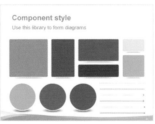

Color palette

Component style

Images overview

Building Presentations Collaboratively

Internet-based presentation applications are becoming more sophisticated every day—and they are free! If you and a colleague or family member need to write a presentation together but work in different locations, you can both work at the same time on the same file! When all the collaboration is done, the file can be viewed online or downloaded to the desktop and presented offline, too.

Add to your album...

On the opposite page, the Google Docs template example on the top row used these doodads for a scrapbook page. They are transparent PNG files that can be overlaid anywhere on a slide for a handmade feel.

Google Docs Template Styles

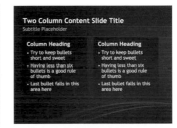

CHAPTER 11

Interacting with Slides

The Power of Constraints

There's not much on this planet more gratifying than being in a healthy and comfortable relationship. My husband and I often use the metaphor of a steamboat to describe our interaction: I'm the one above the surface, sputtering, churning, and making noise to create propulsion; he's the quiet rudder under the surface providing guidance and wisdom to make sure that we don't run aground. I would describe our relationship as interdependent. We rely on and respect what the other brings to the partnership, and that's what makes it successful.

But how would you characterize the relationship you have with your visual aids? What metaphor would you use to describe it? Actor and stage? Or drug and drug user?

When you present, are you codependent, interdependent, or even independent of your slides?

The term codependent was coined in the mid '80s and initially used by Alcoholics Anonymous to describe the unhealthy psychological condition that occurs in a relationship when one partner suffers from an addiction.

A codependent person ends up providing too much care—and often too much latitude—to someone who is unhealthy. You are in a codependent relationship with your slides if you are desperately addicted to them and unable to break away. You may even make excuses for their sad condition, which of course only perpetuates their dilapidated state. If you are in a work culture that enables this codependent relationship, it will be even tougher to transform yourself.

The first step is to admit you have a problem. The second is to acknowledge that your slides have become unmanageable.

Dense content on slides can be addictive. The default template settings in applications such as PowerPoint encourage you to put an enormous amount of text on each slide, which transforms the slide into a document rather than a visual aid. The slides take on the role of teleprompter, requiring you to read them to the audience instead of connecting with your listeners. This habit requires little or no effort on the part of presenters to rehearse; they simply need to read aloud along with the audience. Thus, instead of becoming true "carriers" of your content, you may be happy merely to repeat your own pre-written words. Though definitely the easiest and quickest way to present—it requires no effort on your part other than writing the presentation—is such an approach really best for your audience? It's frustrating to sit through a presentation, reading bullet points, waiting for the presenter to catch up while expanding on the already very thorough and dense text. The audience can read, you know. PSHAW.

Using this medium improperly creates the impression that the presentation is solely about the slides and the presenter, and not about the audience's comprehension or insights. Originally, slides were intended as a visual aid for the audience—a mnemonic device to help them retain and recall the material being presented. Slides are like the stage in a play or the costume for the actor; they are not themselves the star of the show, but they do provide the context and setting in which you can give a memorable performance.

So what can you do if you're trapped in a codependent relationship with your slides that negatively impacts your audience? Garr Reynolds of *Presentation Zen* says that the concept of "restrictions as liberators" can be applied to most any presentation situation. By constraining and restricting yourself and your media, you can break your codependent relationship. But it will take hard work and commitment.

Over the next few pages you'll learn how to constrain your text, the length of your presentation and the output of your projector to help benefit the audience.

Constraining the Text

Letting go of slides-as-crutch is a process that requires time, patience, and practice. Possibly the biggest issue facing presenters is that they don't take the time to rehearse. Think about what a performance would be like if the actors skimmed through the play the night before: it would bomb. Actors spend hours memorizing their scripts and hours more practicing their delivery. That's why they're effective.

Except for me, that is. During sixth-grade summer school I took a theater class and was rewarded for being the last to sign up with the lead role in the play. Instructed to memorize all 36 of my lines, I dutifully attempted to fulfill my task without the benefit of being guided to read the entire play, learn the overarching story line, and appreci-ate the other characters. Rather, I focused on only my lines and remained lost and confused all summer. The plan was to perform the play in front of the entire student body, but we had to have a "special private performance" because of me. Although several lines from that play will be etched in my mind forever, to this day I have no idea what the play was about. I didn't capture the spirit of the story or the meaning of the content. I never ingested it to the point of owning it.

In the end, I couldn't let go of the playbook and needed to carry it around on stage. If only I had been given insights into how to take in the content and make it seem natural and part of me.

Experimenting with letting go of text and slide junk might be hard at first.

That's because when you were writing your presentation you carefully put hundreds of visual triggers on your slides as you formulated the structure and content. As a safety net, you relied on all those triggers to remember to keep your story straight and not screw up your own play. But all those superfluous words and clutter mean nothing to your audience.

The Three R's of Letting Go

Reduce: Practice presenting with your slides a few times. Then, highlight only one keyword per bullet point. Practice delivering those slides again, but focus only on the highlighted word. The other words will still be there, so you can refer to them if needed. Once you can deliver the slides from the keywords, remove all the words on the slides except for the keywords and present from that. Ideally, replace that word with an image when possible, as described on the next page.

Record: Many people are auditory learners. Read your script or present your slides out loud and record the delivery. Play the recording during your commute or close your eyes and listen to it before you go to bed. Once you get past hearing the sound of your own voice, you'll be able to absorb the content and will feel comfortable reducing the clutter on your slides.

Repeat: Read your script, slides, or both out loud several times, and then close your eyes and repeat the content over and over. Or create flash cards, mind maps, or a written summary of your presentation. Repeat, repeat, repeat. In other words, tell yourself your story. Refine it. Get past those stumbling blocks. Then look at your slides and delete as much text and junk as you can while remembering the key points that need to be made.

Removing clutter is a process, one that takes courage, practice, time, and lots of trial and error before you will feel the benefits of being free. You might initially exude more nervous energy when you present, but it will transform your presentations to be more about your connection with the audience and less about the slides. It will also make the world a more attractive place to live.

Reducing Text on a Slide

Remember how scary it was to learn to ride a bike? The first step was getting your mind and body to understand the mechanics of the handlebars. It felt awkward having your feet push the pedals in a circle to turn the wheels that would propel you forward. Getting to this part, though, was relatively easy because you could learn those skills within the safety of the training wheels. It wasn't until you felt comfortable with these new sensations that you either had someone take the training wheels off or bend them up a bit so you could become familiar with wobbling and the concept of self-balancing. You were keenly aware of the risk of falling and getting hurt.

This same fear of failure traps us into not wanting to let go of our heavy text. Letting go is a process, and it takes practice. And yes, possibly falling down. But the practice has a liberating payoff for you and the audience.

Great presenters connect with their audience, speak naturally, and allow the slides to enhance their story.

But that's easier said than done! Memorizing an entire presentation may seem difficult and time-consuming. But it's not as hard as you might think. Here's an exercise to help wean you from the content on your slides.

Learning to Ride

- Put training wheels on the bike
- Raise the training wheels so you wobble
- Wear clothing and a helmet to protect yourself
- Remove the training wheels and practice falling on the grass
- Enjoy riding your bike wherever you need to go

1. Select a slide that has too many words on it.

Learning to Ride

- Put training wheels on the bike
- Raise the training wheels so you wobble
- Wear clothing and a helmet to protect yourself
- Remove the training wheels and practice falling on the grass
- Enjoy riding your bike wherever you need to go

2. Highlight one key word per bullet and rehearse the slide until you can remember all the content when you look only at the highlighted word.

Learning to Ride

- Training wheels
- Wobble
- Clothing
- Grass
- Go!

3. Remove all other text on the slide leaving just the keywords as mnemonics.

Better yet, replace the words on the slide with an image.

Presentation applications have a setting that lets you project an image on the big screen while displaying the notes view on your computer screen. This way you can use your computer screen as the teleprompter or comfort monitor instead of the projected screen.

Navigating Through Your Message
An Interview with Bill McDonough

The first time I worked with McDonough he described for my team the journey he takes his audience on. This method of memorization is sometimes referred to as the Roman Room.

 The ancient Romans used architecture as a mnemonic device for presentations. They would build a structure in their mind and memory that triggered ideas to use in their speech. So as they wandered around in their mental architecture, they would be reminded of various concepts and phrases. I do that same thing. I literally build my speech in my mind with all of its connectivity to ideas, concepts, and details. And then I use all the devices of architecture to create the experience of inhabiting the stories. So if I'm giving a small speech I'll design a baptistery or I'll think of Martin Luther King and his church in Atlanta, or Gandhi sitting and spinning cotton. I focus on one thing that keeps me grounded.

But if I have a big speech, I design a great public building in my mind. It has forecourts and a grand staircase. I'll relate that to the ideas of the storytelling. I'll realize that in order for you to understand this great edifice, I need to take you through a certain series of experiences that are the preamble to entering the building.

When we enter the building I can take you into a vestibule where you'll find yourself in the umbrage. Having come from the great outdoors, your pupils will dilate and you'll try to understand what is going on. In the same way, with the storytelling, at that point I'll bring up one of the central ideas of the story that I want to tell.

But I'll do this in a way that is obscure; not abstruse per se but slightly obscured so you'll wonder what it is I'm talking about. People become quizzical and curious about what they're about to encounter because it's slightly dark, veiled and small, yet it's close and curious. Then I'll walk you into the atrium of the building and all of a sudden it's as bright as day again. But because your pupils are dilated it seems brighter than the outdoors, even though it might be dimmer because you're actually inside a building. The big idea—which is now announced—is as bright as all the great outdoors. And yet you're inside of the building and I have you inside the story.

Each of the rooms off of the atrium will be associated with an idea or a set of ideas. I can wander around the rooms and I can wander out onto a terrace and look at a great view. A great big view might remind me of a great big idea and a geranium in a pot might remind me of another idea, a little idea. I can wander freely.

When I speak without visual aids, I can wander anywhere I want, and I know that I'm not going to lose the story because the story is the building. All I have to do is make sure I get through the whole building and then you've seen the whole story. I can choose different routes. I could decide you're not ready for the kitchen yet so I'm taking you to the living room. I can wander around freely and not lose track of my overall story. When I am using visual aids, I put them in a specific order, the way a tour guide would give you a tour of a building. The slides are in a formatted process.

When we come back out through the atrium you get to see the big idea once more. We go back out through the vestibule, so you go back out through the darkness yet another time. Your curiosity is piqued, then I bring you back to the great outdoors, out in front of the building. All of a sudden the brightness is incredibly bright because now you're back outdoors again and you see the whole world in a different way.

"

(See a case study of Bill McDonough's work on page 30.)

Constraining the Length

Have you ever finished a presentation and had folks flock to you begging you to make it longer next time? Probably not. Attention spans are getting shorter and shorter. Thirty-minute sitcoms, ten-minute YouTube videos, and 15-second commercials all influence the duration of our attention span. And that short span takes into account that TV and Internet media are usually professionally prepared and most often geared to entertain. So, when your content isn't emotionally stimulating but is still crucial and necessary to effective communication, you can enhance the impact by packing punch in a smaller time slot. Dragging the audience down Dullard Lane isn't anyone's favorite afternoon trip.

Constraining your presentation's length forces you to be concise and remove anything superfluous to the message. Proof in point is the recent release of TED videos online (www.ted.com). TED (Technology, Entertainment, Design), an annual conference in California featuring some of the greatest thought leaders and innovators in the world, helps spread ideas and shape our culture and future. We see how each of these phenomenal presenters communicates his or her ideas in 18 minutes or less. So, if some of the most influential people in the world can deliver powerful content in 18 minutes, can you, too. Just try boiling it down.

Another popular presentation technique that uses time as a constraint is Pecha Kucha (see page 228 and www.pechakucha.org). Inaugurated in Tokyo by Klein Dytham architecture and various collaborators, Pecha Kucha brings together designers and thinkers from various industries for an evening of presentations. Each presenter exhibits only 20 slides, each automatically advancing after 20 seconds, for a total of six minutes and 40 seconds of ideas and inspiration.

For internal company meetings, constraining presentations and reserving some of the meeting for conversation, collaboration, and Q&A would be refreshing. Some companies are beginning to constrain the number of slides allowed and encouraging a rapid-fire approach so that more insights can be shared in a single setting.

"Don't you hate it when the presenter has crammed so much information into a presentation that there's no possible way they can get through it all without talking like an auctioneer? They avoid questions and discussion because 'we've got a lot to get through.'

No, we don't.

Presenters bring it upon themselves by trying to cover *Moby Dick, War and Peace,* and *Les Miserables* when we only had time for *One Fish, Two Fish, Red Fish, Blue Fish.*"

Tom Johnson
Author, www.idratherbewriting.com

Just right.

Too many pages of material for one hour.

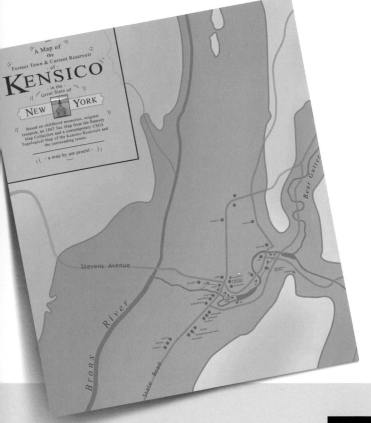

Case Study: Pecha Kucha
Mapping It Out

Pecha Kucha has a quick-paced presentation format of 20 slides, each displayed for 20 seconds, forces the presenter to be a tough editor of their own work. For the audience, it means that boring talks are over quickly and great ones are over too soon. The presenters could be an engaging blend of storyteller, inventor, traveler, illustrator, and map maker. It's an interesting phenomenon to learn so much very quickly from a breadth of resources.

Andy Proehl was one of the presenters at a Pecha Kucha night in San Francisco. He makes maps just for fun, yet his presentation offered enormous insights about design and geography. He grew up near Kensico, NY, and would hear stories that there was a town under the reservoir. There were even rumors that the town's church would stick up out of the water when the water levels were low.

Proehl created a map that combined the old town with the current reservoir. In this image you can see the faint outline of the town near the center confluence of the three valleys.

Here is the town with the reservoir removed. You can see the houses and the names of the people who lived there. Even the church is identifiable.

The top image is of the Kensico Reservoir, north of New York City, and the bottom images are of the town in the 1800s.

Even though only six slides are shown here, you can see how concise and informative they are.

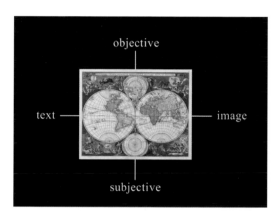

Proehl displayed a matrix to show the dynamic created by these opposing forces. Maps are based on objective data, but it's their subjectivity that makes them interesting. Maps also exist on a continuum between text that is read and images that are viewed.

This map was inspired by Yo Yo Ma's *Silk Road Ensemble.* The Silk Road was defined by its topology. Instead of rendering the map with traditional relief map forms, he used type to show the terrain. The various type forms show the elevation of the mountains through various weights of the type. The Silk Road was like the "Internet of its day" as a vehicle for the spread of goods and ideas.

Constraining the Projector

A further step is to admit you can be PowerPoint-less.

What would it be like to have a relationship independent of slides? Is it possible to deliver a presentation without any slides? Consider what would happen to your presentation if a power outage occurred. Evaluating and rejecting bad habits that have formed from relying on presentation software is critical to your success. It will force you to take ownership of the content in your head and heart.

There are several ways to use visual aids that don't involve a projector. Flip charts, props, handouts, flip books, and even physical devices work if you have a small audience. Using more tactile forms of communication with a small audience increases your humanness. On the other hand, if you are in a large venue with a projector, you can increase your presence by pressing the B key on the keyboard. This will turn your screen to black, forcing your audience to focus on you alternately, the W key will change your screen to white.

Moreover, if your keyboard is out of range, slip an all black slide into your deck. This is equivalent to giving the audience a visual pause.

As you know, if you pause during your presentation, it creates more drama and meaning, and reinforces what you have to say.

Going to black gives the audience time to contemplate. Similarly, turning off the projector during a critical part of your presentation allows the audience to feel as if they are interacting solely with you, which can build credibility and trust.

When in slide show mode, press the B key to turn your screen to black so that focus is on the speaker. Alternatively, press the W key for an all white slide.

All the World's a Stage

When you have an important presentation, the stage can feel bigger than the entire world. It's tough not to notice that the surface area of a projected slide is huge compared to a person. In an average business venue the screen is roughly eight times larger than you and in a large keynote venue with 16:9 aspect ratio, it can be almost 40 times larger than a person. Understandably, this supersized visual dominance puts the focus on the projected images and not the presenter.

Considering that fear of public speaking is ranked higher than the fear of dying, no wonder it's intimidating to walk out on a stage. At Duarte, we've probably seen it all—executives who have ridden motorcycles on-stage (and into the audience), peed their pants, lost consciousness, and even flown us to Comdex to tell them that their hair looks nice in the amber lighting. It's your moment to shine (usually).

16:9 Aspect Ratio

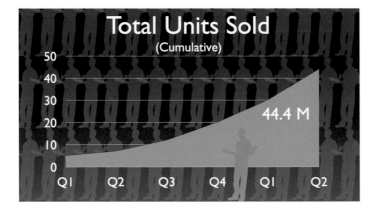

3:4 Aspect Ratio

Many presenters use their slides as an extension of their personas. If their slides look good, they look good. Because it's an in-person medium, some presenters get caught up in "the quality of my slides = the quality of me." This can also be a trap. One year we were hired to create slides for a software conference. The company had no strategy (short or long term) so they had us come in and pretty-up what little they did have. Their presenters were heckled off the stage in some of the sessions.

Sometimes when we work with multiple presenters for the same event, we hear, "Hey, make my slides sexier than John's. I want more pizzazz than him." It's not "I want to have clearer communications"; they want to look better, sexier, jazzier, pizzazier. It's like the slides are an extension of their own persona, looks, and likeability. Your top concern should be how well you communicate, not how good you look. Interestingly, at Duarte, we've only seen this phenomenon with men. We call it slide envy.

Just because your slides look great does not mean they convey useful meaning.

How Many Slides? Use the 10/20/30 Rule.

As a venture capitalist, Guy Kawasaki has to listen to hundreds of entrepreneurs pitch their companies. Most of the pitches are crap: sixty slides about a "patent pending," "first mover advantage," and "all we have to do is get one percent of the people in China to buy our product." So he came up with the 10/20/30 rule for PowerPoint. It's quite simple: a PowerPoint presentation should have 10 slides, last no more than 20 minutes, and contain no font smaller than 30 points. He believes that this rule applies to presentations when the audience needs to reach consensus.

Kawasaki says that 10 slides is the optimal number of slides because a normal human being cannot comprehend more than 10 concepts in a meeting—and venture capitalists are very normal. If you must use more than 10 slides to explain your business, you probably don't have a business.

The Ten Topics That a Venture Capitalist Cares About

① Problem
② Solution
③ Business model
④ Underlying magic/technology
⑤ Marketing and sales

⑥ Competition
⑦ Team
⑧ Projections and milestones
⑨ Status and timeline
⑩ Summary and call to action

You should deliver your 10 slides in 20 minutes. Sure, you have an hour time slot, but you're using a Windows laptop, so it will take 40 minutes to make it work with the projector. Even if setup goes perfectly, people will arrive late and have to leave early. In a perfect world, you give your pitch in 20 minutes, and you have 40 minutes left for discussion.

The majority of the presentations that Guy sees have text in a 10-point font. As much text as possible is jammed into the slide, and then the presenter reads it. However, as soon as the audience figures out that you're reading the text, they read ahead of you. The result is that you and the audience are out of sync.

The reason presenters use a small font is twofold: first, they don't know their material well enough; second, they think that more text is more convincing. Total bozosity. Force yourself to use a point size no smaller 30 points. It will make your presentations better because it requires you to find the most salient points and to know how to explain them well.

This content was slightly modified from Guy's blog at www.guykawasaki.com.

Kawasaki's approach challenges the traditional venture capitalist approach of "walk softly and carry a big deck." This one-size-fits all approach might not work in every situation. VCs being persuaded to part with millions of dollars want to have some content in writing to sink their teeth into and pass around in e-mails. Details and facts are important to them, too—just as important as the clarity of message.

So it's recommended that if you use the 10/20/30 rule, put your script and supporting text into the notes area of your presentation application. If you design your slides and the Notes master layout well, these handouts can be almost as sophisticated as a brochure.

On the next four pages, you'll see other approaches to slide count that work well under different circumstances.

This presentation used images and concepts only with few words. For the handouts afterwards, the notes view was printed two-up so it looked more like a brochure and had all the content available.

And that's when Dr. Thomas discovered the problem with nursing homes—LONELINESS.

He wasn't able to find a cure for Grace's loneliness anywhere in his black medical bag.

He couldn't find a prescription drug that would help.

And none of his medical texts even MENTIONED the word loneliness.

In the end, he had to walk out of Grace's room without being able to ease her suffering, and he returned to his office, determined to find a cure for loneliness.

Then Dr. Thomas started paying closer attention to his other patients.

What he found was heart-breaking. MOST of them were suffering from loneliness. It was widespread in his nursing home, and in every other home he'd visited.

Even worse than that, some of his patients were DYING from loneliness. And if Grace didn't get help soon, he was certain she would join them.

When he realized that loneliness was both widespread and life-threatening, Dr. Thomas called it what it was: a PLAGUE.

Loneliness is the first plague of our Elders.

How Many Slides? The Sky Is the Limit.

When Scott McCloud launched his book *Making Comics*, he took his family on a year-long, 50-state road trip touring and signing books. At each venue, his 13-year-old daughter Sky delivered a presentation. She wasn't intimidated by the standing-room-only crowds; this kid was better than most adults. She had strong delivery skills, commanding stage presence, and a brilliant understanding of the format.

Unbeknownst to her, she used what's been coined as the Lessig Method of presenting. Lawrence Lessig, Professor of Law at Stanford and founder of Creative Commons, employs a signature, fast-paced delivery style with an enormous amount of slides. Each slide has one big idea on it.

So how many slides are right for a presentation? In Sky's short 8-minute talk, she used more than 200 slides, delivered with an engaging cadence.

This quickly paced style isn't easy and requires practice. In fact, it's more common for presenters to display one slide every two minutes. But even that rule of thumb goes only so far. Some presenters require as many as four slides per minute while others will linger on any given slide for four minutes. The point is to use as many slides as you need to get your message across. And please, try to stick with one point per slide. Anything else demands more than most audiences will give.

It was exciting to watch such a young person grasp this communication medium with such authority. Out of the "mouse" of babes comes such great wisdom!

www

Sky McCloud
Daughter of Scott McCloud

How Many Slides? Depends on the Technology.

With the growing popularity of embedding presentations into blogs and social networking sites, presentation repositories like SlideShare.net—the "YouTube of presentations"—are growing exponentially. Anyone can insert a presentation into web-based pages. You can author a presentation once but have it seen by millions of viewers.

The most popular presentations on these sites treat the slides more like a brochure than a slide show. Complete thoughts and phrases are placed on a slide or across a series of slides with simple images. The absence of a presenter requires this graphical style, which is most effective when there's no audio.

Garr Reynolds created a presentation called "Career Advice," based on Dan Pink's book *Johnny Bunko* (you need to own all of Pink's books too). The 184 slides that Reynolds posted on SlideShare take about 6 minutes to read. It's like reading a quick-paced little book that you can review at your own speed.

Obviously Reynolds' style isn't the only format that's successful. But it is engaging and interactive.

Reynolds used a strong design aesthetic by converting the photos to black and white, and then adding a small red element to them.

Because Pink's book is written in a Japanese comic style called Manga, Reynolds incorporated a caricature of himself that popped in and out of scenes.

Some presentations on www.slideshare.net have been viewed by more than a million people. That's enormous reach for a presentation.

To Project or Not to Project

Sometimes the answer is obvious. In a big room, with a big audience, projection is the best. In a small room, with only a couple of people, projecting your slides can seem impersonal.

Now that presentations can be authored once and played on devices, watched on the Web, or printed on paper, you not only need to know the right medium for the audience, but you also must ensure that your content is readable for each screen size. The appropriate medium and size for your presentation are more great reasons why you should invest enough time in your presentation. The one-time investment you make in your presentation could potentially end up being seen across the world.

Slides aren't the only solution for a great presentation. Try to increase the impact of your presentation by changing the visual aids based on the audience.

Flip Chart	Paper Handout	Device	Video

Flip Chart

Small and collaborative settings are best for flip charts. Folks love to see people draw in front of them: there's a wonderment to it. It's rare to see flip charts used in formal settings (but see page 242 for a great example). Flip books are wonderful when only one or two people are sitting with you at a table.

Paper Handout

When the information on the slides is complex or dense, always distribute handouts—preferably at the end of the session so that the audience isn't rustling the paper during your presentation. Also, add an appendix with the extra dense details of data so the audience can verify your facts.

Device

Content that's widely distributed via devices should have accompanying audio and the slides need to be created specifically for this format. Large amounts of text and data don't display well in this format because they're scaled to such a small size.

Video

By either video taping your presentation or transforming your slides to video format, it's easy for your presentation to have a broad web audience. Keep the content short because most video sites have a 10-minute max for videos.

Social Network

Uploading and collaboratively building presentations on the Web allows your presentation to be viewed by anyone in the world. It's a cheap web-conferencing tool. Plus bloggers can insert your presentation into their posts.

Web Cast

Since the viewer sits close to the screen and can move closer to the slides to see details, you can put more text on the screen than when projected. When delivering a presentation where multitasking or distractions are high, break your content into bite-size bursts so the viewer's interest stays piqued.

Projector

In-person presentations can create a moving experience. The screen behind you is huge and slides visually dominate. Live presentations can create powerful energy and electricity in the room, which many times can't be translated when using the other media types shown on this and the previous pages.

Prop

Short for "theatrical property," props typically are ordinary objects. However, a prop must translate well from the stage or when the image is magnified by video feed on the screen. Using a real and tangible item—like showing off a rare object, wearing a funny costume, or revealing a surprise—is a powerful way to drive your point home.

Case Study: John Ortberg
Faith and Flip Charts

After enduring hideous presentations all week at work, the last thing you want to see are bullet points at church. Reading content from bullets in business or educational settings is bad enough, but excerpting them from sacred texts? One example of brilliant use of visual aids doesn't involve slides at all. John Ortberg, Pastor of Menlo Park Presbyterian Church, uses a flip chart. Yes, a flip chart! Even though the congregation has 4,500 members and his sermons are broadcast to two remote locations, the flip chart works! As he speaks, he'll sketch words or images on the flip chart to create a powerful mnemonic that congregants remember throughout the week. It's easy to recall the message because his points are boiled down succinctly into a few key words or a sketch. If he's preaching a series of sermons on the same topic, he'll rewrite the same word series or sketches a few Sundays in a row, just to make sure that his point hits home.

Using a flip chart for a group this size is effective because a video feed magnifies the flip chart on a large screen so that everyone can see it.

The flip chart also provides a means to make his sermons more dynamic and engaging. Best of all, because he writes as he preaches, no one has the chance to read ahead. Pastor Ortberg's flock is captive to his story.

Ortberg uses slides when he refers to scriptures, and the congregants read along with him. When the screens are not in use, beautiful images of nature or stained glass are projected so the congregation can focus on his message.

Even though Ortberg could have used slides in this sermon, he used large signs on easels. He used varying type styles to make each one look like a different type of sign.

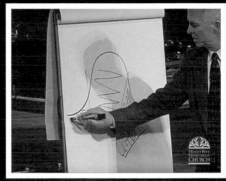

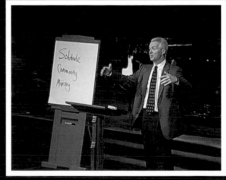

John Ortberg
Pastor, Menlo Park Presbyterian Church

Small Device, Big Impact

Some of the best presenters in the world speak at the TED conference each year. The fascinating thing about attending the conference is that the person sitting next to you sometimes has as great of a story to share as the presenters on the stage.

At one session I sat next to Scott Harrison, founder of charity:water (www.charitywater.org). To describe what he does, he whipped out his iPhone. He related

how he'd been a volunteer photojournalist on board the Mercy Ship *Anastasis* in West Africa. When he returned home in September 2005, he just couldn't stomach the thought of receiving gifts on his birthday. He realized that he didn't need more "stuff." So he asked his friends and family to give their money to help dig freshwater wells in Africa. He then asked them to do the same thing on their own birthdays. Three hundred birthdays later, they'd raised $150,000.

T!P

When converting your presentation to a device like an iPhone, be sure to simplify your content. Onscreen, 24-point type may seem big enough to you, but on the iPhone it reduces to an unreadable 4-point type.

more than
ONE BILLION
people don't have access to
clean, safe drinking water.

the power of
one

Though the message is the same as the Healthy Waters case study on pages 78 to 79, the presentation method differs. Neither method is better than the other, especially if the outcome—safe water for all—is the same.

water changes everything.

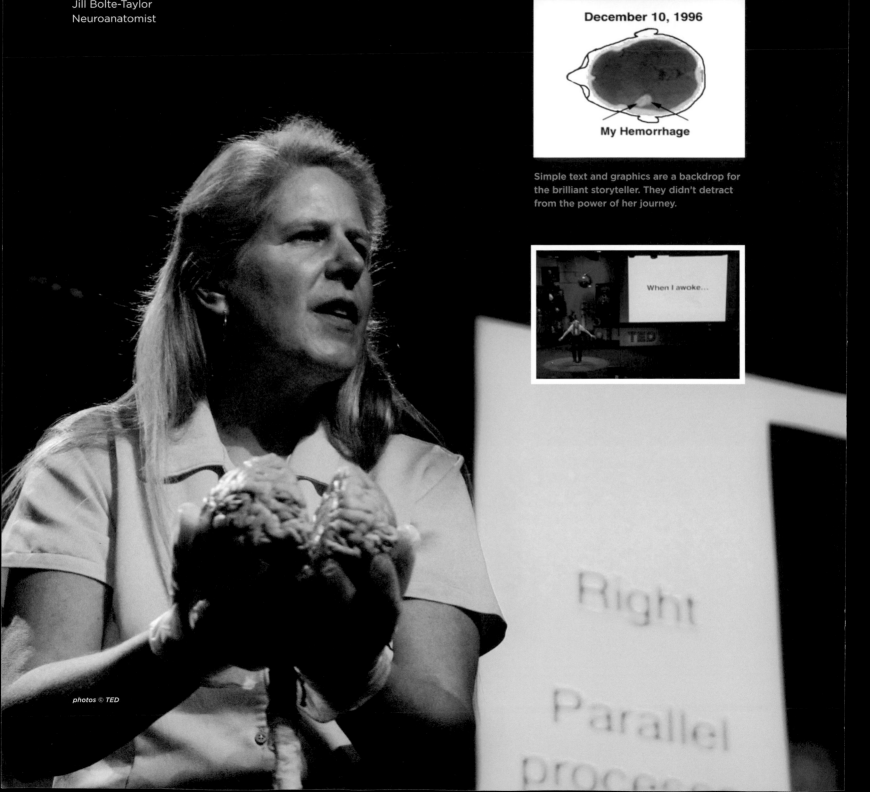

Jill Bolte-Taylor
Neuroanatomist

December 10, 1996

My Hemorrhage

Simple text and graphics are a backdrop for the brilliant storyteller. They didn't detract from the power of her journey.

When I awoke...

Right

Parallel

process

photos © TED

Case Study: Jill Bolte-Taylor
A Stroke of Genius—Fewer Slides

One of the most powerful presentations at TED2008 was that of neuroanatomist Jill Bolte-Taylor, as she described her experience in suffering a stroke. She had a front-row seat to her own brain hemorrhage and we all felt like we were with her as she described what it felt like physically, emotionally, and spiritually.

Use fewer slides. You don't need a ton of slides to create a memorable presentation.

She used only a few slides, huge gestures, and a memorable prop: a real human brain. Her own storytelling skills surpassed the need for media. The slides she did use gave context for why she became a neuroanatomist, what she experienced during her stroke, and how it changed her life.

To hear her incredible story, view the presentation at www.ted.com.

Bolte-Taylor used huge gestures to describe feelings of euphoria as the left side of her brain shut down.

She contracted her gestures when she described how she'd surrendered her spirit and was ready to transition out of this world.

A Call to Relate

Presentations are a very human medium. And that's what sets them apart. It's you. You are unique. You are the only one like you from anywhere for all time. You have your own fingerprint, your own experiences and your own story that can be told like no one else can tell it. Your passion is your own and its expression can only come from you.

Creating a movement or change is hard. But you are the only one who expresses the way you do and your way of expressing will resonate in the hearts and minds of others.

Many passionate change-agents have altered the arts, industries, and the world. Martha Graham shaped a new expression in dance when she tapped into her soul and brought her own unique expression to the art.

Many who came to see Martha were moved deeply even though she didn't say a word. What she expressed on the stage touched lives and connected with the way she exposed her soul while she danced.

"There is a vitality, a life force, a quickening that is translated through you into action, and there is only one of you in all time. This expression is unique, and if you block it, it will never exist through any other medium; and be lost. The world will not have it. It is not your business to determine how good it is, not how it compares with other expression. It is your business to keep it yours clearly and directly, to keep the channel open. You have to keep open and aware directly to the urges that motivate you. Keep the channel open. No artist is pleased. There is no satisfaction whatever at any time. There is only a queer, divine dissatisfaction, a blessed unrest that keeps us marching and makes us more alive than the others."

Martha Graham

Great presenters strive to be both personal and multi-dimensional. Presentations are delivered both verbally and visually. It's also a medium of contradictions. When you're live, you have the opportunity to build relation-ships with your audience. Unfortunately, the format encourages us to become automatons, using slides as a metronome to deliver prescribed information, often with your back to the people you're trying to reach. In reality, you need to come across like a real person, and presentation applications don't inherently facilitate this.

Ultimately, the healthiest relationship to have with your slides is one of interdependence. It's not just about finding a balance with your slides; there is a third party in this relationship—the audience. So, instead of using the media to showcase yourself and your dependencies, the audience should be able to see what you're saying.

Presentations are a wonderful medium to express your passion. You get to be human and connect with an audience emotionally and analytically.

As you look at the faces in the audience, you can see the response to your message in their faces. If they feel like they've been enlightened, moved to act, or made willing to change their behavior, you've been successful.

Next time you give a presentation, consider a different approach—look at your content through the eyes of the audience. Take them on your journey by showing them something they've never seen before. Employ great stories, reveal convincing information, and communicate in your own, genuinely human way.

CHAPTER 12

Manifesto: The Five Theses of the Power of a Presentation

Treat Your Audience as King

They didn't come to your presentation to see you. They came to find out what you can do for them. Success means giving them a reason for taking their time, providing content that resonates, and ensuring it's clear what they are to do.

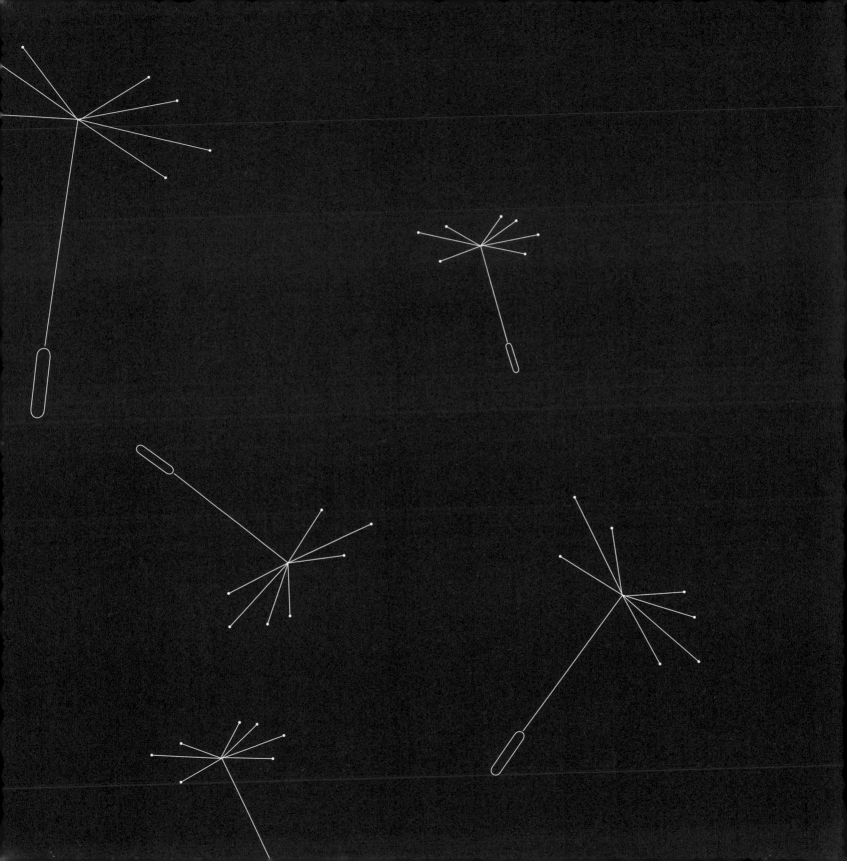

Spread Ideas and Move People

Creating great ideas is what we were born to do; getting people to feel like they have a stake in what we believe is the hard part. Communicate your ideas with strong visual grammar to engage all their senses and they will adopt the ideas as their own.

Help Them See What You're Saying

Epiphanies and profoundly moving experiences come from moments of clarity. Think like a designer and guide your audience through ideas in a way that helps, not hinders, their comprehension. Appeal not only to their verbal senses, but to their visual senses as well.

Practice Design, Not Decoration

Orchestrating the aesthetic experience through well-known but oft-neglected design practices often transforms audiences into evangelists. Don't just make pretty talking points. Instead, display information in a way that makes complex information clear.

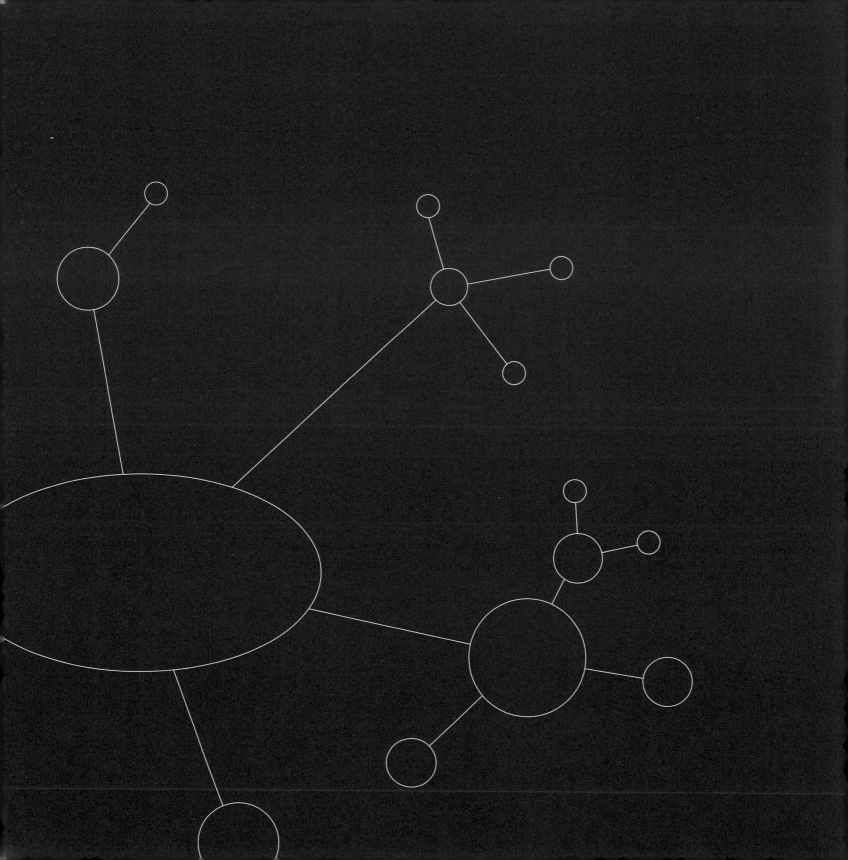

Cultivate Healthy Relationships

A meaningful relationship between you, your slides, and your audience will connect people with content. Display information in the best way possible for comprehension rather than focusing on what you need as a visual crutch. Content carriers connect with people.

References

The following material has influenced the design and business
practices of Duarte. Please add these to your library also:

Design

Bajaj, Geetesh, and Echo Swinford. 2007. *Microsoft Office PowerPoint 2007 Complete Makeover Kit.* Que Publishing.
Before and After Magazine. http://www.bamagazine.com.
Block, Bruce. 2007. *The Visual Story, Second Edition: Creating the Visual Structure of Film, TV and Digital Media.* Focal Press.
Communication Arts Magazine. http://www.commarts.com.
Critique Magazine. (out of print). http://www.critiquemagazine.com.
Godin, Seth. 2001. *Really Bad PowerPoint.* http://www.sethgodin.com/freeprize/reallybad-1.pdf.
Harrington, Richard, and Scott Rekdal. 2007. *How to Wow with PowerPoint.* Peachpit Press.
Krause, Jim. 2003. *Designers Complete Index.* North Light Books F+W Publications, Inc., How Design Books.
Lidwell, William, Kritina Holden, and Jill Butler. 2003. *Universal Principles of Design.* Rockport Publishers, Inc.
Mayer, Richard E. 2001. *Multimedia Learning.* Cambridge University Press.
Reynolds, Garr. 2008. *Presentation Zen: Simple Ideas on Presentation Design and Delivery.* Peachpit Press, New Riders.

Branding

Aaker, David A. 1996. *Building Strong Brands.* Simon & Schuster, Ltd.
Neumeier, Marty. 2006. *The Brand Gap.* Peachpit Press, New Riders.

Visual Thinking

Neumeier, Marty. 2006. *Zag: The Number One Strategy of High-Performance Brands.* Peachpit Press, New Riders. Arnheim, Rudolf. 1972. *Visual Thinking.* (out of print). University of California Press.
Horn, Robert E. 1999. *Visual Language: Global Communication for the 21st Century.* MacroVU, Inc.
McAlhone, Beryl, and David Stuart. 1998. *A Smile in the Mind.* Phaidon Press Inc.
Pink, Daniel H. 2006. *A Whole New Mind: Why Right-Brainers Will Rule the Future.* Riverhead Trade; Penguin Group (USA) Inc.
Roam, Dan. 2008. *The Back of the Napkin: Solving Problems and Selling Ideas with Pictures.* Portfolio / Penguin Group (USA) Inc.

Information Graphics

Harris, Robert L. 2000. *Information Graphics: A Comprehensive Illustrated Reference.* Oxford University Press.
Heller, Steven. 2006. *Nigel Holmes on Information Design.* Jorge Pinto Books, Inc.
Holmes, Nigel. 2005. *Wordless Diagrams.* Bloomsbury USA Publishing.
Pedersen, B. Martin. 1988. *Graphis Diagram 1.* (out of print). Graphis Press Inc.
Wurman, Richard Saul. 1990. *Information Anxiety.* Doubleday Books.
Wurman, Richard Saul. 1999. *Understanding USA.* TED Conferences.

Data Display

Few, Stephen. 2006. *Information Dashboard Design: The Effective Visual Communication of Data.* O'Reilly Media, Inc.
Few, Stephen. 2004. *Show Me the Numbers: Designing Tables and Graphs to Enlighten.* Analytics Press.
Tufte, Edward R. 2006. *Beautiful Evidence.* Graphics Press.
Tufte, Edward R. 1990. *Envisioning Information.* Graphics Press.
Tufte, Edward R. 2003. *The Cognitive Style of PowerPoint.* Graphics Press.
Tufte, Edward R. 1983. *The Visual Display of Quantitative Information.* Graphics Press.

Content

Atkinson, Cliff. 2007. *Beyond Bullet Points.* Microsoft Press.
Decker, Bert. 2005. *Creating Messages That Motivate.* Lightning Source Inc.
Heath, Chip and Dan Heath. 2007. *Made to Stick: Why Some Ideas Survive and Others Die.* Random House, Inc.
University of Chicago Press. 2003. *The Chicago Manual of Style.* University of Chicago Press.

Business Books

Bossidy, Larry, Ram Charan, and Charles Burck. 2002. *Execution: The Discipline of Getting Things Done.* Crown Business.
Collins, Jim. 2006. *Good to Great.* Arrow Books Ltd. HarperCollins.
Flamholtz, Eric G., and Yvonne Randle. 2007. *Growing Pains: Transitioning from an Entrepreneurship to a Professionally Managed Firm, 4th Edition.* Jossey-Bass.
Gerber, Michael E. 1999. *The E-Myth Manager: Why Most Managers Don't Work and What to Do About It.* HarperCollins.
Kawasaki, Guy. 2004. *The Art of the Start.* Portfolio.
McGhee, Sally. 2007. *Take Back Your Life!: Using Microsoft Outlook to Get Organized and Stay Organized.* Microsoft Press.
Robert, Michel. 1993. *Strategy Pure and Simple.* McGraw-Hill, Inc.
Trout, Jack. 2001. *Differentiate or Die.* Wiley.

Index

Join the conversation.
digitalmedia.oreilly.com

comprehensive tutorials   informative podcasts   technical articles   shortcuts   recipes   forums

O'REILLY®